THE FIRST CASUALTY

THE TRUTH ABOUT THE AMERICAN INVASION OF AFGHANISTAN

JOHN ADAM & M. A. AKBAR

Strand Non fiction

Copyright © 2009 John Adam & M. A. Akbar

The right of John Adam & M. A. Akbar to be identified as the authors of this work has been asserted in accordance with the Copyright, Designs and Patents Act 1988.

All rights reserved. No reproduction, copy or transmission of this publication may be made without written permission. No paragraph of this publication may be reproduced, copied or transmitted save with the written permission or in accordance with the provisions of the Copyright Act 1956 (as amended.) Any person who does any unauthorised act in relation to this publication may be liable to criminal prosecution and civil claims for damage.

First published 2009 by Strand Publishing UK, Ltd.

Golden Cross House, 8 Duncannon Street, Strand,

London WC2N 4JF

E-mail address: info@strandpublishing.co.uk

Internet address: www.strandpublishing.co.uk

Paperback ISBN 978-1-907340-03-1

'In war, truth is the first casualty'
Aeschylus

THE FIRST CASUALTY

The First Casualty

Afghanistan, a landlocked country, occupies a strategic position in the region due to its geographical location. Afghanistan has a long experience of power struggles for dominance and has seen many ups and downs in its history. Many nations have exploited the importance of Afghanistan for their own vested economic, military and strategic interests. Thus, the Afghanistan issue is a very complex one, little understood in the West, or not understood at all. The devastation suffered by this nation - if indeed it can be properly called a nation - is unique in history. War has followed war, as inevitably, it seems, as day follows night. This rivalry has resulted in ever-increasing instability in the entire region.

To understand Afghanistan fully - or even partially, for the situation has always been complex – it is necessary to have been there. The present writers know the country well. Every invader from Alexander the Great long ago to the Americans and their allies today has discovered that a major factor in any attempted conquest of Afghanistan is the terrain. This is a country of precipitous mountains and deep defiles, of wide rivers, torrents when the rains come, and many nullahs, or small streams. No commander can be unaware of the terrain as a central factor in his strategy.

Command and control of the heights is the central factor in frontier warfare as it not only affects observation and survey but also gives psychological ascendancy, no mean factor when troops are under stress in often severe climatic conditions. Such terrain causes constriction on mobilisation and has channelising effects. Security of main supply routes is vital for success of any operation.

Movement in the mountains necessitates decentralization of command and control, and this in turn calls for increased responsibility and initiative, not least at junior officers' level, though in some cases the leaders may be senior non-commissioned officer. Whoever is the leader, it is clear that looking for orders from central command is not likely to breed any measure of success.

In such terrain there is always the threat of ambush. We read in newspaper or hear in the non-print media of ambushes and wonder why trained soldiers should be so caught. The answer is the nature of the terrain. To prevent ambush, it is necessary to use troops in order to protect convoys. And when an ambush occurs, as they do, evacuation of casualties and stores can be slow, because there is no central command structure.

Although there are rivers and nullahs in abundance, there is, ironically, often a shortage of water, by which we mean safe drinking water. Sustenance of soldiers has a direct bearing on the duration of an operation and the quantum of force. And if this were not irony enough, heavy rains often result in roads being blocked by mudslides and such, which also creates problems for routine operational logistics.

The First Casualty

Anyone who has tried to use a mobile cell phone in hilly country knows that signal reception can be poor, intermittent or not available at all. In terrain such as is found in Afghanistan, this question of communication is compounded several times. Mountains and defiles screen signals, necessitating support systems for VHF sets. A patrol that is not only cut off from its company by distance but also by lack of adequate communications systems is always vulnerable.

Of course, the nature of Afghanistan and the neighbouring regions of Pakistan also have effects on the opposition, the enemy. The very country that hampers large troop numbers being deployed lends itself to the success of small-scale guerrilla operations. There is no better place to hide than in mountainous regions such as Tora Bora, as Osama bin Laden proved in the early stages of the American attack on Afghanistan, and as the Soviets learned in their ten-year war against the *mujahideen*. In the dry season what better route to use for infiltration than a dry or black nullah?

In such terrain major roads cannot be constructed in a straight line. They must, of necessity, wind through valleys which are themselves dominated by mountain ranges. Thus there are opportunities in many places for guerrillas to set up an ambush of a military convoy or a civilian convey under military protection. In such conditions roadside bombs have proved most effective.

The First Casualty

Once again the terrain affects patterns of habitation. In such country there are more small villages and hamlets than there are large towns. The Taliban and their Al-Qaeda allies gain support from the people of the villages. Indeed they could not long operate successfully without such support and sustenance. This lesson was learned in Vietnam and also in the *chimurenga* the struggle for victory in Zimbabwe. The people of the villages are asked to provide for the Taliban and do so. They have no choice. And when government or allied troops enter a village the man who was a Taliban fighter can quickly merge with the population and appear to be a farmer working in his fields.

In such circumstances when politicians and generals talk rather glibly of winning the hearts and minds of the Afghan people this is for public consumption in the United States and in the countries of its many UN and NATO allies. Given the nature of the terrain and, given the weakness of central government in Kabul, it should come as no surprise to anyone that the people give their allegiance to a local clan leader or to a tribal warlord, for such leaders are able to provide protection in exchange for allegiance. It is the social contract in its purest form. Unless you can protect, you will never win hearts and minds.

'In war, truth is the first casualty'. Thus wrote Aeschylus, the Greek dramatist, two and a half thousand years ago. It was true then; it is true now. Separating truth from propaganda is never easy but in this book we are trying to

The First Casualty

get at the facts.

<>

It all started, it seems and we add the note of doubt deliberately, on 11 September 2001 and the story was simple, or so it appeared to the general public. Terrorists had hijacked four commercial jet planes and attempted to fly them into several U.S. targets. Whatever we may think of the great loss of life and the destruction of buildings it has to be admitted that the strategy was brilliant and had been planned carefully and in sophisticated ways. The United States was supposedly dealing with some backward mountain people living in the vastnesses of Afghanistan and Pakistan. Yet it did not seem so. This was a brilliant coup, a strike at the very heart of the most advanced and powerful nation on earth. Two aeroplanes were deliberately piloted into the Twin Towers of the World Trade Center in New York. People all over the United States and in many other countries around the world watched the events on television as they happened, or saw re-runs later that same day. There was no other news. The United States had been attacked at its very heart.

An attack on the Pentagon in Washington DC resulted in comparatively minor damage. Another was brought down in a field by sustained passenger resistance, with loss of life. But another plane, American Airlines Flight 11, was deliberately smashed into Tower One of the World Trade Centre at 8:50 AM. United Airlines Flight 175 struck -

The First Casualty

again deliberately - Tower Two at 9:04 AM. As the world watched on television, Tower Two collapsed to the ground at about 10:00 AM. This scene, unforgettable to those who saw it, was duplicated at 10:30 AM when Tower One also crumbled and crashed to the ground. This attack brought about the death of approximately three thousand men, women and children, from many nations around the world, for such is the cosmopolitan nature of New York's population.

The people of America joined together in common outrage, disbelief and deep grief. It is hard to grieve for those we do not know but the graphic pictures shown on television seemed to bring the horror close into the hearts of the American people and their allies in other countries around the world. How was it possible for two aircraft to penetrate air space right at the heart of the world's greatest commercial city? At few times in their brief history have the American people been so united and this was in many ways a re-run of their collective feeling after the Japanese attack on Pearl Harbor in 1941, which heralded American entry into World War 11. People responded with donations of blood, effort and money. Shock and grief were seen clearly on the faces of the American people.

President George W Bush immediately called for all civilized nations, as he said, to join together and fight terrorism. The military of the United States was mobilized for war in an operation called *Enduring Freedom,* a name with a hopeful and defiant ring to it. What the president

The First Casualty

did not tell the world and dare not tell the world was that this was no bolt out of the blue. There had been attacks on US embassies in Kenya and Tanzania. There had been strikes against *USS Cole* in port at Aden on the southern coast of Yemen. There were even rumours of troop movement in countries to the north of Afghanistan, former Soviet republics, now independent Muslim states striving for survival.

It was 12 October 2000. *USS Cole,* a destroyer under the command of Commander Kirk Lippold, entered Aden harbour for a routine fuel stop. *USS Cole* completed mooring at 09:30. Refuelling started one hour later, at 10:30. At around 11:18 local time a small craft approached the port side of the destroyer and an explosion occurred, putting a 40-by-60-foot gash in the ship's port side. The blast appeared to be caused by explosives placed against the hull of the boat. At the time there was speculation that more than 1,000 pounds of explosive were used. The blast hit the ship's galley, where crew were waiting in line for lunch.

The blast caused extensive damage. The crew had to fight flooding in the engineering sections. Divers inspected the hull and determined that the destroyer's keel had not been damaged. However, seventeen American sailors had been killed and thirty-nine others injured in the blast. The wounded were taken to the United States Army's Landstuhl Regional Medical Center near Ramstein, Germany and later flown back to the United States. The

The First Casualty

attack was the deadliest against a U.S. Naval vessel since the Iraqi attack on the *USS Stark* on 17 May 1987.

It was concluded that the attack had been planned, directed and executed by a terrorist organisation known as Al-Qaeda and that the leader of this group, or network of groups, was Osama bin Laden. A video recording of Osama bin Laden showed him boasting about the success of the attack on *USS Cole* and encouraged other individuals and groups to plan and execute other attacks on the United States.

The next attack, bigger in scale than *USS Cole*, more adventurous and ambitious, and certainly successful, was that of 9/11.

The people of the United States came together. At least, this was how the media expressed it. The hard truth was that there were already divisions within the United States. Support for President George Bush was not overwhelming. There were deep controversies within the country, not least Bush's decision of March 1993 to send troops into Iraq. The reasons given for the invasion of Iraq were clear and commanded much support in the United States and Britain. Countries such as France were lukewarm however. President Bush, who as president is also commander-in-chief, claimed that Iraq was developing weapons of mass destruction and also giving aid to Al-Qaeda. These allegations were never proved. Indeed, many people came eventually to the conclusion

The First Casualty

that to invade Iraq and remove Saddam Hussein, the leader of the country, was a monumental error. Saddam was no democrat, no Arab leader ever was, but he was a secularist and had established control over a diverse and unruly people - Arabs and Kurds - and was no danger to the Western allies.

In Britain, Prime Minister Tony Blair was a fervent ally of George Bush. In its wish to carry the electorate with it Blair's government peddled lies about weapons of mass destruction. Those who opposed the invasion of Iraq, and there were many – though not among the main Conservative opposition in parliament – were branded as unpatriotic. In the event no weapons of mass destruction were ever found, and the electorates of both the United States and the United Kingdom reached the conclusion that their respective governments had lied deliberately, had set out to hoodwink. Even the masses of people who find television programmes of utter banality more interesting than politics - more interesting even than the death of soldiers in battle – aroused themselves briefly and expressed opposition to the invasion. Opponents of the war in Iraq came from right across the political spectrum and the reasons for opposition were many. There was, however, a general view that the invasion of Iraq was primarily intended for the purpose of gaining for the Allies a foothold in the Middle East. Of course, more than a foothold, an entire country. Many felt strongly that to attack Iraq was a sideshow merely a deliberate attempt to divert public attention from the real centre of hostilities, which was now in Afghanistan. Since 9/11 there had been a hunt for Osama and his comrades, mainly in the Tora Bora mountain regions, but he had eluded capture and has continued to do so up to almost one decade later.

Once the Allies had invaded Afghanistan the defeat of the Taliban did not take long, as we have noted. The Taliban has, however, since re-grouped and once again become a formidable force – not perhaps in open warfare, for that is rare in any war these days, but in frustrating the Allied efforts to extend full control over such renegade provinces as Helmand. What was not quickly concluded was the capture and trial of Osama bin Laden. That would have been a major coup for George Bush, but it was not to be. Indeed, it has never been classified.

One month after the events of 11 September, 2001 George W. Bush, President of the United States from 2001 to 2009, identified Osama Bin Laden as the chief suspect in the attacks. Bin Laden was known to be in Afghanistan, and Afghanistan at that time had a government led by the Taliban. If much of what we know of Al-Qaeda remains shrouded in mystery and enigmatic, our knowledge of the Taliban is much clearer. It is a political movement with its roots in Sunni Islam, tends to be fundamentalist in its Islamic beliefs and is composed mainly of men from the Pashtuns. It is known not to favour education for girls and women, and seeks stricter codes of law and behaviour, based – it is claimed – on Sunni Islam. The Taliban governed Afghanistan from 1996 until 2001, when a swift

The First Casualty

American-led invasion, Operation Enduring Freedom, removed it from power in Kabul. From what seemed utter defeat, the Taliban has, however, re-grouped and is currently waging war, and often successfully, against the government in Kabul, forces from NATO, (the ISAF), the Americans, and often against neighbouring Pakistan.

So it was in September 2001, while the whole of the United States seemed still to be in mourning and shock, President George W Bush made several demands that he insisted the Taliban government must accept and execute forthwith. The Taliban must:
- deliver Al-Qaeda leaders located in Afghanistan to the United States authorities;
- release all imprisoned foreign nationals, including American citizens;
- protect foreign journalists, diplomats, and aid workers in Afghanistan
- close terrorist training camps in Afghanistan and 'hand over every terrorist and every person and their support structure to appropriate authorities';
- allow access by Americans to training camps, in order to verify their closure.

These were harsh demands of any government to make of another sovereign nation, but the times were not normal, and, as we shall see presently, George Bush needed a reason to enter Afghanistan and topple the Taliban, as well as seeking out Osama bin Laden and his associates.

The First Casualty

'They will hand over the terrorists or they will share in their fate,' said President Bush, speaking to the American Congress in Washington. 'Our war on terror begins with Al-Qaeda, but it does not end there.'

The Taliban government was not one to sit down quietly in the face of threats, but knowing the military power of the United States and its allies, it decided to make what was, in the circumstances, quite a conciliatory response. The response was sent through the Afghanistan embassy in Islamabad the capital of Pakistan. There was no evidence of which they were aware that linked Osama bin Laden to the September 11 attacks in America. It was also stated that bin Laden was a guest in their country and that Pashtun and Taliban codes of behaviour require that all guests be granted hospitality, which was probably the first such response in diplomatic history.

On 22 September, 2001 the United Arab Emirates and then Saudi Arabia, both of whom had previously recognised the Taliban as the legitimate government of Afghanistan, withdrew recognition – no doubt at the insistence of the American government - leaving Pakistan as the only country with diplomatic ties to the Taliban regime.

On 7 October, 2001 before the onset of military hostilities, the Taliban offered to bring bin Laden to an Islamic court in order to assess if he were guilty or not. This offer was rejected. The very same day the United States and British planes carried out bombing raids. The war had started.

The First Casualty

Nobody believed that it would be over by Christmas; though the removal of the Taliban from Kabul was swift and it appeared that the movement had been destroyed or at least dispersed.

What is likely, and what is less well known, is that U.S. Army Rangers were training special troops inside Kyrgyzstan, and there were reports - unconfirmed but likely, given what we know of political and military deceit - that Tajik and Uzbek special troops were being trained in the American states of Alaska and Montana even before the attack on the Twin Towers. The United States was determined to invade, despite their knowledge of the ten year Soviet involvement and ultimate defeat. The Russians had claimed at the time that they were making a tactical withdrawal, but everyone knew it was a defeat.

The plan, initially, was to attack from the north, from Uzbekistan and Tajikistan. The latter country was deemed to be especially important strategically. The United Nations Security Council did not authorize *Operation Enduring Freedom*, as the United States grandly and optimistically termed the invasion. According to the Americans, UN authorization for the invasion was not legally required because this was an act of national self-defence and not aggression; but even if UN sanction had been legally necessary, under the UN Charter, the Americans, in belligerent mood, would doubtless have gone ahead anyway. There was no declaration of war. This was an incursion to capture terrorists, not soldiers. This being so, those captured were transferred to Guantanamo Bay, an American enclave in Cuba. The United States had assumed territorial control over the base under the 1903 Cuban-American Treaty, which granted the United States perpetual lease of the enclave. Because the detainees sent there from Afghanistan were considered to be terrorists, and not soldiers, they did not have the rights and protection afforded to soldiers; they did not come under the provisions and protection of the Geneva Convention.

Two months later, on 20 December, 2001 the United Nations Security Council authorized the creation of an International Security Assistance Force - ISAF - with authority to assist the Afghan Interim Authority in Kabul in maintaining, as far as possible, law and order. In August 2003, command of ISAF passed to the North Atlantic Treaty Organization (NATO). This was fiction: everyone knew that actual control was in the hands of the Americans, senior partner in any Western alliance.

After initial bombing, the ground offensive commenced. The first ground troops were from the Central Intelligence Agency's Special Activities Division. They were soon joined by U.S. Army Special Forces from the 5th Special Forces Group. These combined groups led the Northern Alliance intended to overthrow the Taliban. This was achieved without the deployment of conventional U.S. forces. Strikes were made on Kabul, at the airport; the city of Jalalabad; and on Kandahar, home of Mullah Omar, leader of the Taliban. An attempt was made to soften

The First Casualty

liberal criticism with an announcement that while the Taliban would be targeted, as would terrorist training camps, at the same time food and medical supplies would be dropped to alleviate suffering by the civilian population of the country.

The declared aim of the invasion was to find Osama bin Laden and other high-ranking Al-Qaeda leaders members, bring them to trial, and thus destroy the whole organization of Al-Qaeda. The secondary purpose was to destroy the Taliban regime, which had afforded safe haven to Al-Qaeda. The Bush doctrine stated that it would not distinguish between terrorist organisations and nations or governments that harboured them. It was the age-old dictum: you are either for us or against us. There was, it seemed, no place for neutrality.

In a pre-recorded videotape Osama bin Laden was in jaunty mood. The United States, he declared, would fail in Afghanistan, just as the Soviets had done earlier. It is on record that bin Laden believed events in Afghanistan had been the prime cause of the collapse of the Soviet Union. The collapse of the United States could also be achieved.

The International Security Assistance Force (ISAF) was established by the UN Security Council and placed under NATO command. The ISAF now has almost seventy thousand soldiers, provided by 41 countries. This is a coalition that even the Allied coalition of WW2 cannot rival, at least in terms of countries involved.

The First Casualty

The countries with troops in ISAF include:
- United States 31,855
- Britain 9,000
- Germany 4,250
- France 3,070
- Canada 2,830
- Italy 2,795
- Netherlands 2,160
- Poland 2,025
- Australia 1,200
- Spain 1,000
- Romania 990
- Turkey 820
- Denmark 700
- Norway 600
- Belgium 510
- Bulgaria 460
- Sweden 430
- Czech Republic 340

TOTAL 65,030
Other nations: 2,670

ISAF TOTALS: 67,700
ADDITIONAL US TROOPS 33,000

GRAND TOTAL **100,700**

(Sources: Reuters; U.S. military; NATO

The First Casualty

(www.nato.int/isaf/docu/epub/pdf/isaf_placemat.pdf)

These are figures for October 2009, the time that we are writing. This is a US and British war. The figures make it obvious that - for all the fiction of ISAF and United Nations Security Council sanction - this is an American invasion, with the United Kingdom as its principal ally.

To this date, Osama bin Laden has not been found. He could be in many countries: Pakistan, in the tribal areas; in Saudi Arabia, where he was born; in Yemen, which outside of the main cities of Sana'a, Aden and Taiz is not controlled by the central government; or he could, perhaps, be dead. So, who is, or was, Osama bin Laden.

<>

Osama bin Laden was born in Riyadh, Saudi Arabia. In an interview in 1988 he gave his date of birth as 10 March 1957. His father Muhammed Awad bin Laden was a wealthy businessman with ties to the Saudi royal family. Osama bin Laden was born the only son of Muhammed bin Laden's tenth wife. Soon after the child's birth the parents divorced. The mother then married again and Osama lived in the new household with three stepbrothers and one step-sister.

Bin Laden was raised as a devout Wahhabi Muslim. He studied economics and business administration at King Abdul Aziz University. Reports of his academic

The First Casualty

achievement vary: some sources claim that he earned a degree in civil engineering in 1979; others that it was public administration and he graduated in 1981. There are also sources that suggest he dropped out in his third year. What appears to be agreed is that while at university bin Laden's main interest was religion.

In 1974, at the age of 17, he married his first wife. Again, sources vary in respect of wives and children. Some suggest four women and 25 or 26 children, while others talk of between 12 and 24. Either way, he clearly did not spend his whole time reading within religion.

Bin Laden believes that the restoration of Sharia law will set things right in the Muslim world and that all other ideologies have to be opposed. He believes Afghanistan under the rule of Mullah Omar's Taliban to be the one true Islamic country and has consistently dwelt on the need for violent jihad to right what he believes are injustices against Muslims perpetrated by the United States. There is a need to wipe Israel from the map. Gambling, usury, homosexuality, the taking of drugs, including alcohol, cannot be permitted. Osama is no friend of democracy in any form.

Probably the most infamous and loathsome part of Bin Laden's ideology is that civilians, including women and children, are legitimate targets of jihad. He is anti-Semitic, and has warned against alleged Jewish conspiracies. Nor are all Muslims spared: Shia Muslims have been listed

The First Casualty

along with heretics, the United States and Israel as the four enemies of Islam. Music has no place in his world view, but killing thousands of civilians in the name of jihad is acceptable.

Osama Bin Laden had been living in Afghanistan along with other members of Al-Qaeda, operating training camps having an alliance with the Taliban. How strong this alliance was has never been made clear. When, in 1998, U.S. embassies in Africa were attacked, with significant loss of life, notably in Kenya, the US military responded by launching cruise missiles at these camps. How effective these strikes were, in terms of limiting Al-Qaeda activities, is also unknown.

In the next two years the United Nations, usually a dilatory organisation, a mere talking shop and that is to express it mildly, issued Resolutions 1267 and 1333. These resolutions were specifically aimed at the Taliban. Sanctions, financial and military, were threatened. The purpose was to persuade the Taliban to hand over Osama bin Laden for interrogation and trial in relation to the Africa bombings. It was also intended that training camps in Afghanistan should be closed. If the Taliban failed to arrest bin Laden and hand him to the United States military, the United States would consider itself at war with the Taliban or anyone who aided or gave encouragement to Al-Qaeda.

◇

The First Casualty

After 9/11, as the destruction of the Twin Towers became universally known, the United States was at war. Part of the strategy was to use force to remove the Taliban government in Afghanistan. Regime change, as such strategies became known. If this necessitated giving assistance to the enemies of the Taliban within the country, so be it. Again, a famous dictum of *Realpolitik* comes to mind: 'My enemy's enemy is my friend'. One of the enemies of the Taliban was the Northern Alliance. Because of the great distances involved, the United States needed bases close to Afghanistan. These were found in India and Russia, and especially in Uzbekistan and Tajikistan. It was from the latter country – a former state of the Soviet Union, now independent – that the United States intended to invade Afghanistan. The objectives were simple: to apprehend Bin Laden and his associates; and to effect regime change in Afghanistan. It could not be simpler. In the real world of politics, however, nothing is ever simple. Wars do not solve problems; they produce even more problems, without solving the original one.

Bombers operating at high altitudes, well out of range of anti-aircraft fire, bombed Al-Qaeda training camps and Taliban air defences. During the initial build-up preceding the actual attack, there had been speculation in the media that the Taliban might try to use U.S.-built Stinger anti-aircraft missiles. If any of these missiles existed at the time of the air campaign, they were never used and the U.S. did not lose any aircraft to enemy fire. U.S. aircraft,

The First Casualty

including Apache helicopter gunships, operated with impunity throughout the campaign.

The strikes initially focused on the area in and around the cities of Kabul, Kandahar and Jalalabad. Within the short time of a few days, training sites were severely damaged and the Taliban's air defences destroyed. To make it difficult for the Taliban to communicate, command, control, and communication targets were attacked. Despite this, the Taliban line opposed to the Northern Alliance remained intact. Two weeks into the campaign, the Northern Alliance demanded the air campaign focus more on the front lines. Meanwhile, thousands of Pashtun militiamen based in Pakistan crossed into Afghanistan to join their fellows. In any event, the frontier between the tribal areas of the two countries has never been strongly demarcated; the terrain does not permit this.

The war was well planned and appeared to be going according to plan. The next stage of the campaign began with carrier based F/A-18 Hornet fighter-bombers hitting Taliban vehicles in pinpoint strikes, while other U.S. planes began cluster bombing Taliban defences. After years of fighting, the Northern Alliance smelled success. The Taliban support structure began to erode under the pressure of the air-strikes. U.S. Army Special Forces judged the time was right to launch an audacious ground raid deep into the Taliban's heartland of Kandahar, even striking one of Mullah Omar's compounds.

The First Casualty

At the beginning of November the Taliban front lines were relentlessly bombed with 15,000-pound bombs and by AC-130 helicopter gunships. The Taliban fighters had no previous experience of such sustained fire power as the Americans produced, not even in the ten years of Soviet occupation, and they were unsure of how to respond, if indeed they could respond. This was a war of what the Americans had promised in Iraq – one of shock and awe. By 2 November, Taliban frontal positions had been broken; the Northern Alliance was poised to take Kabul. As the Taliban collapsed, so Al-Qaeda fighters took over security in the Afghan cities. What made the Afghan campaign a landmark in the military history of the United States was that Special Operations forces from all the services, along with Navy and Air Force tactical power, prosecuted it. Other operations by the Afghan Northern Alliance and the CIA were equally important and fully integrated. No large army or marine forces were initially deployed. During these early months of the war the U.S. military had a limited presence on the ground. The plan was that Special Forces, and intelligence officers with a military background, would serve as liaisons with Afghan militias opposed to the Taliban, who would advance after air power had destroyed the Taliban.

Intelligence reports identified the Tora Bora Mountains, which lie roughly east of Afghanistan's capital Kabul - itself close to the border with Pakistan – as the place where bin Laden and his commanders were hiding. American intelligence analysts believed that the Taliban

The First Casualty

and Al-Qaeda had dug in behind networks of fortified caves and underground bunkers. The area was subjected to a heavy and almost continuous air bombardment by B52 bombers. In one of the caves, it was believed, were Osama bin Laden and his commanders. To the Northern Alliance, it seemed that the main American objective was the capture of Osama and his henchmen and their subsequent trial. For the Northern Alliance, on the other hand, the main objective was to take over the government of the country from the discredited and defeated Taliban.

On 5 November General Abdul Rashid Dostum - generally accepted as the leader of the Uzbeks living in Afghanistan and himself a former pro-Soviet supporter in the Russian invasion - led the Uzbek faction in an attack on the towns of Keshendeh-bala, Keshendeh-pane and various other strongholds within the Darya Suf Valley south-west of Mazar-i-Sharif, seizing them with the assistance of U.S. Special Operators and with his horse-mounted troops. But, it was in the town of Bai Beche that the tide began to turn with the death of a key Taliban commander, the capture of another and the destruction of 150 troops during a battle that lasted twelve hours. At the same time, 2000 Tajik forces, moved south. The city of Mazir-i-Sharaf, on the road to Kabul, was about to fall. Reprisals by the Northern Alliance that had suffered at the hands of the Taliban were feared. The country has over many centuries witnessed savage reprisals. No group or clan has clean hands.

Al-Qaeda did not sit still. They moved 4,000 fighters

The First Casualty

across country to organise a defence of Mazir-i-Sharif. The battle commenced with American Special Forces launching precision bombing on selected targets. Taliban and Al-Qaeda commanders, living in bunkers, were especially targeted. And yet, the Taliban boasted they could hold the city.

Mazar-i Sharif was considered important, not only because it is the home of the Shrine of Azar Ali or Blue Mosque, a site sacred to Islam, but also because it is the location of two airports and also a major road that leads into Uzbekistan. Its capture was vital to the Allied effort. On November 9, Northern Alliance forces, under the command of Generals Dostum and Mohammed Door, - Uzbek and Tajik respectively - swept across the Pu-i-Imam Buckhorn bridge, meeting little resistance, and seized the city's main military base and airport. American Special Forces were also in the field. In wars, strange bedfellows lie down together, against what is perceived to be a common enemy. The fall of the city of Mazar-i-Sharif was swift, and soon the Taliban and Al-Qaeda were in retreat. The defenders of Mazar-i-Sharif included fighters who were Chechen, Pakistani, Uzbek, Chinese Muslims, and not a few Arabs who had come specially to Afghanistan to defend the country against what they considered infidel invaders.

Withdrawal from the city began. The Northern Alliance forces entered the city from the Balk Valley, meeting only light resistance. By sunset, the majority of the Taliban

The First Casualty

forces had retreated to the north and east, in an attempt to mass for a counter-attack. It was later estimated that 400-600 people had died in the battle; approximately 1,500 Taliban were captured or chose to defect to the opposition. The capture of Mazar-i-Sharif on Friday 9 November – a mere two months since the destruction of the Twin Towers – represented the first substantial victory of the campaign. For the Allies it was a considerable propaganda coup.

Upholding the claim by Taliban officials that they would be able to move 500 fresh fighters into the city, as many as 900 Pakistani fighters reached Mazar-i-Sharif in the following days as the majority of the Taliban were evacuating. It was claimed later that many of these young men were recruited by a Pakistani Mullah, Sufi Mohammed, who used a loudspeaker riveted to a truck to broadcast that 'Those who die fighting for God don't die! Those who go on jihad live forever, in paradise!'

For almost two days as the group, led by a large number of Chechen and Arab sympathisers, gathered in the abandoned Sultan Razia Girls' School building. It is somewhat ironic that a government so fiercely opposed to the education and advancement of females, should make a stand in a girls' school. Town officials and leaders of the Northern Alliance attempted negotiations for their surrender, but the fighters vehemently refused, ultimately killing two peace envoys, a town mullah and his military escort. All the while they constantly fired at anyone who moved within the vicinity of the building, including civilians drawn to the scene out of curiosity. For several it was to be a lethal curiosity. After the murders of the envoys, the Northern Alliance began returning fire on the school but with little immediate effect. This gun battle continued for several hours. Inside the battered school, someone scrawled on the walls the words of their mullah: 'Die for Pakistan' and 'Never Surrender.' By mid-afternoon it had been decided to dislodge the defenders by bombing them. Planes were called in. The compound was obliterated.

The capture, occupation and holding of Mazar-i-Sharif had significant strategic importance: supply routes were again open; there was an airstrip for humanitarian aid via U.S. airlifts as well as deliveries by relief organizations to hungry people in the countryside. This aid alleviated Afghanistan's looming food crisis, which had threatened more than six million people with starvation. A large proportion of those in most urgent need lived in rural areas to the south and west of Mazar-i-Sharif.

Then rumours started to circulate that Mullah Dadullah was moving towards the city in command of 8,000 Taliban soldiers. Dadullah was a Pashtun and senior military commander of the Taliban until his death, at the age of about forty-one, in 2007. He was a handsome and charismatic commander with several victories to his credit. Therefore, in response to this very real threat, one thousand American troops were rushed to the defence of the city. This was easier, because the Americans now had

The First Casualty

their own air base from which to launch air strikes, compared with formerly when they had to scramble from as far away as Uzbekistan or from aircraft carriers in the Arabian Sea, that warm water that the Tsars had so coveted, and the Soviets after them. The expected counter-offensive did not materialise, but Mullah Dadullah continued to lead a busy and often brutal life. It is, perhaps, worth noting that Dadullah had lost a leg fighting with the American-supported mujahideen against Soviet occupation in the 1980s. Before the American invasion in 2001, the year that the country joined the Great Game, Dadullah had been on the central council of the Taliban, in effect the parliament of Afghanistan. Not that the Taliban would have set up anything resembling a western-style parliament.

The American-backed forces now controlling the city began broadcasting music, which had been banned by the Taliban for the past five years. Songs were introduced by a female announcer, another major breakthrough, for women had since 1996 been prohibited from education, work and many other civil liberties, even liberties of the most basic kind. Compared with the West, where the advancement of women has in recent years been rapid, even with women occupying positions of power such as prime minister – Margaret Thatcher, Angela Merkel - or secretary of state – Condoleeza Rice - the Taliban wanted a return to feudal times. Of course, much of the thinking of extreme Muslims has a medieval cast.

The First Casualty

The next city to fall was the capital, Kabul. On the night of 12 November Taliban forces fled from the city, leaving under cover of darkness. By the time Northern Alliance forces arrived in the afternoon of 13 November only bomb craters and destroyed gun emplacements were there to greet them but there was a group of about twenty hard-line Arab fighters hiding in the city's park. All members of the group were killed in a fifteen-minute gun battle. The capital had been secured, but Mullah Dadullah escaped to carry on the fight in another way or on another day, which assuredly he did until his death in 2007. Dadullah had been a central figure in the recruitment of Pakistani nationals to the Taliban and was also one of the main Taliban spokesmen, frequently meeting Al-Jazeera television reporters. In the summer of 2006 he was reportedly sent by Mullah Omar to South Waziristan to convince local Pashtun insurgents to agree a truce with Pakistan. It was even rumoured that in 2006, as part of a deal for reconciliation, Dadullah – who instigated the capture and murder of hostages – would be made Minister of Defence. All he had to do was come in from the cold.

However, in May 2007 Mullah Dadullah was killed after a raid on his HQ. Involved in the raid were Afghan and NATO troops, and also a British unit known as the Special Boat Squadron, or SBS, who at the time were operating in Helmand province. Dadullah's younger brother became military leader of the Taliban.

◇

The First Casualty

To return to the initial invasion, the fall of Kabul marked the collapse, at least for the time being, of the Taliban. It was widely believed that they could not possibly re-group as a strong fighting force. This, alas, has not proved to be the case. The return to the battle of the Taliban has been perhaps the major surprise of the whole campaign. Within twenty-fours hours of the fall of Kabul to NATO and Northern Alliance troops, all of the Afghan provinces along the Iranian border, including the key city of Herat, had fallen. Local Pashtun commanders and warlords had taken over throughout north-eastern Afghanistan, including the key city of Jalalabad. The Taliban, aided by Pakistani volunteers, fell back on the northern town of Kunduz, where 10,000 Taliban fighters, led by foreign fighters, refused to surrender and continued to put up resistance. Meanwhile, American Special Forces scoured the caves of the Tora Bora complex, but failed to find Osama bin Laden. Had he been captured, this would have been a major coup for the Americans, but it was not to be, and the war continued, with the Taliban recovering quickly and again joining the fight. There were successes for the Allies. Al-Qaeda leader Mohammad Atef was killed in an air strike in November, 2001. The attack also killed other high ranking Al-Qaeda personnel.

Just as the bombardment at Tora Bora was increasing, the siege of Kunduz was continuing. Finally, after nine days of heavy fighting and heavy American aerial bombardment, Taliban fighters surrendered to Northern

Alliance forces on November 25-November 26. Shortly before the surrender, Pakistani aircraft arrived ostensibly to evacuate a few hundred intelligence and military personnel who had been in Afghanistan previous to the U.S. invasion for the purpose of aiding the Taliban's ongoing fight against the Northern Alliance. However, during this airlift, it is alleged that up to five thousand people were evacuated from the region, including Taliban and Al-Qaeda troops allied to the Pakistanis in Afghanistan. This operation remains a mystery, and it is doubtful if more than a few individuals know the whole story. What is true, for certain, is that the Pakistan ISI was deeply involved. But who or what is ISI? What is the history and what are the purposes of this branch of Pakistan security? A short diversion is in order.

◇

After independence in 1947, two new intelligence agencies were created in Pakistan: the Intelligence Bureau (IB) and the Military Intelligence (MI). However, the weak performance of the MI in sharing intelligence between the Army, Navy and Air Force during the Indo-Pakistani War of 1947 led to the creation of the Directorate for Inter-Services Intelligence (ISI) in 1948. The ISI was structured to be manned by officers from the three main military services, and to specialize in the collection, analysis and assessment of external intelligence, either military or non-military. The ISI was the brainchild of Australian-born British Army officer, Major General R.

The First Casualty

Cawthorn, then Deputy Chief of Staff in the Pakistan Army. Initially, the ISI had no role in the collection of internal intelligence, with the exception of the North-West Frontier Province and Azad Kashmir.

The objectives of ISI from the beginning have been to:
- safeguard Pakistani interests and national security inside and outside the country.
- monitor the political and military developments in adjoining countries, which have direct bearing on Pakistan's national security and in the formulation of its foreign policy and to collect foreign and domestic intelligence in such cases.
- co-ordinate the intelligence functions of the three military services.
- keep vigilant surveillance over its cadre, foreigners, the media, politically active segments of Pakistani society, diplomats of other countries accredited to Pakistan and Pakistani diplomats serving outside the country.

In the late 1950s, when Ayub Khan became the President of Pakistan, he expanded the role of ISI in safeguarding Pakistan's interests, monitoring opposition politicians, and sustaining military rule in Pakistan. The ISI was reorganised in 1966, after intelligence failures in the Indo-Pakistani War of 1965 and expanded in 1969. Khan entrusted the ISI with the responsibility for the collection of internal political intelligence in East Pakistan. Later on, during the nationalist revolt in Balochistan in the mid

The First Casualty

1970s, the ISI was tasked with performing a similar intelligence gathering operation.

The ISI lost its importance during the regime of Zulfiqar Ali Bhutto, who was very critical of its role during the 1970 general elections, which triggered off the events leading to the partition of Pakistan and the emergence of Bangladesh.

After General Zia ul-Haq seized power in July 1977, the ISI was expanded by making it responsible for the collection of intelligence about the Sindh based Communist party and various political parties such as Bhutto's Pakistan Peoples Party (PPP).

The Soviet-Afghan war of the 1980s saw the enhancement of the covert action capabilities of the ISI by the U.S. Central Intelligence Agency (CIA). A special Afghan Section was created under the command of Colonel Mohammed Yousaf to oversee the coordination of the war. A number of officers from the ISI's Covert Action Division received training in the US and many covert action experts of the CIA were attached to the ISI to guide it in its operations against the Soviet troops by using the Afghan Mujahideen.

◇

One of the least discreditable actions of the Americans, in league with ISI, was to allow the evacuation of Taliban,

The First Casualty

Al-Qaeda and others from Afghanistan to Pakistan when Kunduz was about to fall to the Northern Alliance. This was in November 2001. Victorious Northern Alliance troops swept into Kunduz shooting wounded prisoners and leaving them to die in the city's marketplace as they ended a two-week resistance by Taliban forces in their last stronghold in northern Afghanistan.

Hopes of a peaceful end to the stand-off were shattered as Northern Alliance soldiers embarked on house-to-house searches looking for hidden Taliban forces. Up to 5,000 Taliban fighters were said to have surrendered, some of whom were hauled away in trucks with their arms tied behind their backs with scraps of cloth. And in scenes that fed criticisms of the Alliance, and of Washington's support for them, the fly-covered bodies of three Afghan Taliban fighters were left on empty stalls in Kunduz's marketplace. Residents claimed that the men were captured after they were wounded in fighting and, contrary to all rules of war, shot dead by Alliance soldiers. Yet it has been claimed that there was an accord between the Taliban and the Northern Alliance for Taliban forces to submit peacefully. Under the accord, the Afghan Taliban were meant to be granted an amnesty. If this is true, and there is no reason to doubt it, it seems that the Northern Alliance was more bent on revenge than on accord. Foreign fighters, mainly Pakistani, Chechens and Saudis, were to be imprisoned and tried.

The Alliance defended its conduct, saying that its forces

met resistance as they entered the city. Fierce fighting broke out at daybreak as the main contingent of Alliance troops entered the city. It would appear that Taliban forces ambushed the Alliance soldiers with gunfire and rocket-propelled grenades. Thousands of Alliance troops, rushed into the city, fought back. They admitted that their forces had killed around 100 Taliban in street fighting. What followed was carnage, and the claim of one hundred dead Taliban seems to be a deliberate underestimate.

The scenes of violence, that have been called a massacre, have been used by critics of the Alliance, who see it as a brutal organisation that has no interest in bringing together Afghanistan's rival ethnic groups. After the vengeful reprisals and the scenes of violence the Alliance was jubilant as it celebrated the capture of Kunduz after a two-week siege. Some observers said the city's defenders - even foreign volunteers expected to fight to the death - were laying down their weapons.

It was, as a correspondent for the UK newspaper *The Guardian* reported on 16 November, 2001, 'richly ironic that the first achievement of the war on terrorism has been to install in Kabul the Northern Alliance, for whom terrorism has been the entire line of business and way of life for more than 20 years.'

At a press conference in Kabul the Northern Alliance said that it now controlled the city of Kunduz but was still facing 'pockets of resistance' to the west. Thousands of

The First Casualty

Taliban soldiers and Arab fighters were giving themselves up, said Abdullah Abdullah, the Alliance foreign minister. 'In one area there are 2,000 Taliban including foreigners who have surrendered to the joint commission,' he said. 'They left behind their tanks and heavy armour and surrendered their weapons.'

Ali Razim, an adviser to the Alliance commander General Rashid Dostam, said that 5,000 Taliban had eventually surrendered to his forces. Most were locals who were released. But 750 Taliban, who were suspected of being foreigners, were imprisoned at General Dostam's base near Mazar-i-Sharif.

A group of Arab supporters of Osama bin Laden were reported to have broken out of Kunduz and fled to the nearby town of Chardara, just west of Kunduz. The Alliance claimed that they were encircled, with nowhere to run.

The fall of Kunduz, after a siege lasting three weeks, ended - at least for the time being - the Taliban's presence in northern Afghanistan allowed American bombers to concentrate their fire power on Mullah Omar's stronghold of Kandahar. A spokesman for the Pakistan foreign ministry, Aziz Ahmed Khan said that prisoners who surrender should be treated in accordance with international law. He said Pakistan had asked the UN and the Red Cross to try to find out whether there were any Pakistanis among the dead in Mazar-i-Sharif.

The First Casualty

Truth is indeed the first casualty of war. What was not known at the time, save to a few, was that the Americans had connived with Pakistan to allow the escape of several Taliban and Al-Qaeda notables and fighters. This was, it appears, at the behest of General Pervez Musharaff, President of Pakistan at that time. The original request by General Musharraf was to President George Bush, but Dick Cheney – gung ho vice-president - took charge. The approval was not shared with anyone, not even with Colin Powell, Secretary of State, until well after the event. President Musharraf said Pakistan needed to save its dignity and its valued people.

Two planes were involved. They made several sorties per night over several nights. They took off from air bases in Chitral and Gilgit in Pakistan's northern areas, and landed in Kunduz, where the evacuees were waiting on the tarmac. Certainly hundreds and perhaps as many as one thousand people escaped. Hundreds of ISI officers, Taliban commanders, and foot soldiers belonging to the IMU and Al-Qaeda personnel boarded the planes. American officers watching from surrounding high ground dubbed this evacuation as Operation Evil Airlift.

A senior American diplomat later claimed the United States had been fooled by Musharaff., but this was not pursued further. However, at the time nobody wanted to hurt Musharraf; his prestige with the Pakistan army was at stake. The real question is why Musharraf did not get his

The First Casualty

men out before. The ISI, it seemed, was running its own war against the Americans and did not want to leave Afghanistan until the last moment. Some have suggested that President Musharraf gained American support for the airlift by warning that the humiliation of losing hundreds - perhaps thousands - of Pakistani military men and intelligence operatives would jeopardize his political survival. Musharaff was America's man, it seemed, and there was great willingness to assist him. Many of the people evacuated were the Taliban leadership who Pakistan hoped could play a role in a post war Afghan government. In the game of political poker this was a strong card in Musharraf's hand; hence the secret evacuation. No one should ever be surprised at the chicanery of politicians.

By the very nature of such operations, it is difficult to cite actual evidence. It is even harder to arrive at the full truth. For those who wish to delve deeper, the following secondary sources may be of assistance.

Newsweek 16/11/2001 & 11/8/2002; Los Angeles Times 16/11/2001' New York Times 30/09/2002;

Michel Chossudovsky of the Centre for Research on Globalization – www.globalreseach.com

The Times of India has gone further, suggesting on 24 January 2002 that it was not Taliban and Al-Qaeda moderates who might be expected to participate in a

The First Casualty

government of national reconciliation in Afghanistan, but the hard core of these two allied movements.

While there may be truth that President Musharaff wanted to get his ISI people out safely, we tend to accept the cock-up theory. Such was the tumult of those nights that Taliban and Al-Qaeda people found a place on aircraft not because of some dire plot in Islamabad, but simply because of the confusion that prevailed.

On 25 November, the day that Taliban fighters holding out in Kunduz surrendered and were being herded into the Qala-i-Janghi fortress near Mazar-i-Sharif, a few Taliban attacked some Northern Alliance guards, taking their weapons and opening fire. This incident soon triggered a widespread revolt by 300 prisoners, who soon seized the southern half of the complex, once a medieval fortress, including an armoury stocked with small arms. One American CIA operative who had been interrogating prisoners, Johnny Spann, was killed, marking the first American combat death in the war. Or perhaps we should say second, for we know that truth is always the first casualty.

The revolt was finally put down after seven days of heavy fighting between an SBS unit along with some US Army Special Forces and Northern Alliance, AC-130 gunships and other aircraft took part providing strafing fire on several occasions, as well as a bombing air strikes. Of the Taliban, 86 prisoners survived and around 50 Northern

The First Casualty

Alliance soldiers were killed. The quashing of the revolt marked the end of the combat in northern Afghanistan where local Northern Alliance warlords were now firmly in control.

By the end of November, Kandahar, the movement's birthplace, was the last remaining Taliban stronghold and was coming under increasing pressure. Nearly 3,000 tribal fighters, led by Hamid Karzai, a westernised and polished loyalist of the former Afghan king, and Gul Agha Sherzai, the governor of Kandahar before the Taliban seized power, together put pressure on Taliban forces from the east and cut off the northern Taliban supply lines to Kandahar. The threat of the Northern Alliance loomed in the north and north-east. Meanwhile, the first significant U.S. combat troops had arrived. Nearly 1,000 Marines, ferried in by CH-53E Super Stallion helicopters, set up a Forward Operating Base known as Camp Rhino in the desert south of Kandahar on 25 November. This was the coalition's first strategic foothold in Afghanistan and was the stepping-stone to establishing other operating bases. The first significant combat involving U.S. ground forces occurred a day after Rhino was captured when 15 armoured vehicles approached the base and were attacked by helicopter gunships, destroying many of them. Meanwhile, air strikes continued the pounding of Taliban positions inside the city, where Mullah Omar was holed up. Omar, the Taliban leader, remained defiant despite the fact that his movement only controlled four out of the 30 Afghan provinces by the end of November. As commanders in tight corners will, he called on his forces to fight to the death.

As the Taliban were weakened, so the American focus homed in on the Tora Bora. Local tribal militias, numbering over 2,000 strong and paid and organized by Special Forces and CIA paramilitaries, continued to mass for an attack as heavy bombing continued of suspected Al-Qaeda positions. 100-200 civilians were reported killed when 25 bombs struck a village at the foot of the Tora Bora and White Mountains region. On 2 December, a group of 20 U.S. commandos was inserted by helicopter to support the operation. On 5 December, Afghan militia wrested control of the low ground below the mountain caves from Al-Qaeda fighters and set up tank positions to blast enemy forces. The Al-Qaeda fighters withdrew with mortars, rocket launchers, and assault rifles to higher fortified positions and dug in for the battle.

By 6 December, Omar finally began to signal that he was ready to surrender Kandahar to tribal forces. His forces had been broken by heavy U.S. bombing and living constantly on the run within Kandahar to prevent himself from becoming a target. In such circumstances even Mullah Omar's morale lagged. Recognizing that he could not hold on to Kandahar much longer he began signalling a willingness to enter into negotiations to turn the city over to the tribal leaders, assuming that he and his top men would receive some protection. The U.S. government rejected any amnesty for Omar or any Taliban leaders. On

The First Casualty

7 December, Mullah Mohammad Omar slipped out of the city of Kandahar with a group of his hardcore loyalists and moved northwest into the mountains of Uruzgan Province, reneging on the Taliban's promise to surrender their fighters and their weapons. He was last reported seen driving off with a group of his fighters on a convoy of motorcycles. Other members of the Taliban leadership fled into Pakistan through the remote passes of Paktia and Paktika Provinces.

Nevertheless, Kandahar, the last Taliban-controlled city, had fallen, and the majority of the Taliban fighters had disbanded. The border town of Spin Boldak was surrendered on the same day, marking the end of Taliban control in Afghanistan. The Afghan tribal forces under Gul Agha seized the city of Kandahar while American Marines took control of the airport outside and established a U.S. Base.

Al-Qaeda fighters were still holding out in the mountains of Tora Bora, however, while an anti-Taliban tribal militia steadily pushed bin Laden back across the difficult terrain, supported by powerful air strikes guided in by U.S. and UK Special Forces. Facing defeat, the Al-Qaeda forces agreed to a truce to give them time to surrender their weapons. In retrospect, however, many believe that the truce was a ruse to allow important figures, including Osama bin Laden, to escape. The Allies closed all roads except one and that allowed a walk of about eight to ten hours to the border with Pakistan. It is likely that Osama

The First Casualty

walked this road.

On 12 December, fighting flared again, probably initiated by a rear guard buying time for the main force's escape through the White Mountains into the tribal areas of Pakistan. Once again tribal forces backed by British and U.S. special operations troops and air support pressed ahead against fortified Al-Qaeda positions in caves and bunkers scattered throughout the mountainous region. By 17 December, the last cave complex had been taken and their defenders overrun. A search of the area by U.S. and UK forces continued into January, but no sign of bin Laden or the Al-Qaeda leadership emerged. It is almost unanimously believed that they had already slipped away into the tribal areas of Pakistan to the south and east. It has been estimated that around 200 of the Al-Qaeda fighters were killed during the battle, along with an unknown number of anti-Taliban tribal fighters. No U.S. or UK deaths were reported.

Meetings of various Afghan leaders were organized by the United Nations Security Council and took place in Germany. The Taliban were not included. These meetings produced an interim government and an agreement to allow a United Nations peacekeeping force to enter Afghanistan. The UN Security Council resolutions of 14 November, 2001 included 'Condemning the Taliban for allowing Afghanistan to be used as a base for the export of terrorism by the Al-Qaeda network and other terrorist groups and for providing safe haven to Osama bin Laden,

The First Casualty

Al-Qaeda and others associated with them, and in this context supporting the efforts of the Afghan people to replace the Taliban regime.'

The UN Security Council resolution 20 December, 2001, 'Supporting international efforts to root out terrorism, in keeping with the Charter of the United Nations, and reaffirming also its resolutions 1368 (2001) of 12 September, 2001 and 1373 (2001) of 28 September, 2001.'

Before the U.S.-led invasion, there were fears that the invasion and resultant disruption of services would cause widespread starvation and refugees. The United Nations World Food Programme temporarily suspended activities within Afghanistan at the beginning of the bombing attacks but resumed them after the fall of the Taliban. It was estimated that the productive valleys could, in the absence of hostilities, produce up to 30,000 tons of cereals annually. By November 1 U.S. C-17s flying at 30,000 feet (30,000 feet) had dropped 1,000,000 food and medicine packets marked with an American flag.

Following Tora Bora, U.S. forces and their Afghan allies consolidated their position in the country. Following a Loya jirga or grand council of major Afghan factions, tribal leaders, and former exiles, an interim Afghan government was established in Kabul under Hamid Karzai. U.S. forces established their main base at Bagram airbase just north of Kabul. Kandahar airport also became an important U.S. base area. Several outposts were established in eastern provinces to hunt for Taliban and Al-Qaeda fugitives. The number of U.S-led coalition troops operating in the country would eventually grow to over 10,000. Meanwhile, the Taliban and Al-Qaeda had not given up. Al-Qaeda forces began regrouping in the Shahi-Kot mountains of Paktia province throughout January and February 2002. A Taliban fugitive in Paktia province, Mullah Saifur Rehman, also began reconstituting some of his militia forces in support of the anti-U.S. fighters. They totalled over 1,000 by the beginning of March 2002. The intention of the insurgents was to use the region as a base area for launching guerrilla attacks and possibly a major offensive in the style of the Mujahideen who battled Soviet forces during the 1980s.

U.S. allied to Afghan militia intelligence sources soon picked up on this build-up in Paktia province and prepared a massive push to counter it. On 2 March 2002 U.S. and Afghan forces launched an offensive on Al-Qaeda and Taliban forces entrenched in the mountains of Shahi-Kot southeast of Gardez. The jihadist forces, using small arms, rocket-propelled grenades and mortars, were entrenched into caves and bunkers in the hillsides at an altitude that was largely above 10,000 feet (3,000 metres.) They used hit and run tactics, opening fire on the U.S. and Afghan forces and then retreating into their caves and bunkers to weather the return fire and persistent U.S. bombing raids. To render much worse the situation for the coalition troops, U.S. commanders initially seriously underestimated the Taliban and Al-Qaeda forces as a last isolated pocket numbering fewer than 200. It turned out that the guerrillas numbered between 1,000-5,000 according to some estimates and that they were receiving reinforcements, not least from sympathisers from Pakistan and some of the old Soviet republics.

By 6 March, eight Americans and seven Afghan soldiers had been killed and reportedly 400 opposing forces had also been killed in the fighting. The coalition casualties stemmed from a friendly fire incident that killed one soldier, the downing of two helicopters by rocket-propelled grenades and small arms fire that killed seven soldiers, and the pinning down of U.S. forces being inserted into what was coded as *Objective Ginger* that resulted in dozens of wounded. However, several hundred guerrillas escaped the dragnet, and headed to the Waziristan tribal areas across the border in Pakistan.

During Operation Anaconda and other missions during 2002 and 2003, some special forces from several western nations were also involved in operations. These included the Australian Special Air Service Regiment, the Canadian Joint Task Force 2, the German KSK, the New Zealand Special Air Service and Norwegian Marinejegerkommandoen.

Following the battle at Shahi-Kot, it is believed that the Al-Qaeda fighters established sanctuaries among tribal protectors in Pakistan, from which they regained their strength and later began launching cross-border raids on

U.S. forces by the summer months of 2002. Guerrilla units, numbering between 5 and 25 men, still regularly crossed the border from their sanctuaries in Pakistan to fire rockets at U.S. bases and ambush American convoys and patrols, as well as Afghan National Army troops, Afghan militia forces working with the U.S-led coalition, and non-governmental organizations. The area around the U.S. base at Shkin in Paktika province saw some of the heaviest activity.

Meanwhile, Taliban forces continued to remain in hiding in the rural regions of the four southern provinces that formed their heartland: Kandahar, Helmand Province, Uruzgan and Zabul. In the wake of Operation Anaconda The Pentagon requested that British Royal Marines, highly trained in mountain warfare, be deployed. A number of missions were conducted over several weeks. The results varied. The Taliban, who during the summer of 2002 numbered in the hundreds, avoided combat with U.S. forces and their Afghan allies as much as possible and melted away into the caves and tunnels of remote Afghan mountain ranges or across the border into Pakistan during operations.

After managing to evade U.S. forces throughout mid-2002, the remnants of the Taliban gradually began to regain their confidence and started to begin preparations to launch the insurgency that Mullah Muhammad Omar had promised during the Taliban's last days in power. During September, Taliban forces began a recruitment drive in

The First Casualty

Pashtun areas in both Afghanistan and Pakistan to launch a renewed 'jihad' or holy war against the Afghan government and the U.S-led coalition. Pamphlets distributed in secret during the night also began to appear in many villages in the former Taliban heartland in southeastern Afghanistan that called for jihad. Small mobile training camps were established along the border with Pakistan by Al-Qaeda and Taliban fugitives to train new recruits in guerrilla warfare and terrorist tactics, according to Afghan sources and a United Nations report. Most of the new recruits were drawn from the madrassas or religious schools of the tribal areas of Pakistan, from which the Taliban had originally arisen. Major bases, a few with as many as 200 men, were created in the mountainous tribal areas of Pakistan by the summer of 2003. The will of the Pakistani paramilitaries stationed at border crossings to prevent such infiltration was called into question, and Pakistani military operations proved of little use.

The Taliban gradually reorganized and reconstituted their forces over the winter, preparing for a summer offensive. They established a new mode of operation: gathered into groups of around 50 to launch attacks on isolated outposts and convoys of Afghan soldiers, police, or militia and then breaking up into groups of 5-10 men to evade subsequent offensives. U.S. forces in the strategy were attacked indirectly, through rocket attacks on bases and improvised explosive devices. To coordinate the strategy Mullah Omar named a 10-man leadership council for the resistance with himself at the head. Five operational zones were created and assigned to various Taliban commanders such as the key Taliban leader Mullah Dadullah in charge of Zabul province operations. Al-Qaeda forces in the east had a bolder strategy of concentrating on the Americans, planning and executing elaborate and increasingly lethal ambushes.

The first sign that Taliban forces were regrouping came on 27 January 2003 during Operation Mongoose, when a band of fighters allied with the Taliban and Hezb-i-Islami were discovered and assaulted by U.S. forces at the Adi Ghar cave complex 15 miles (24 km) north of Spin Boldak. 18 rebels were reported killed and no U.S. casualties reported. The site was suspected to be a base to funnel supplies and fighters from Pakistan. The first isolated attacks by relatively large Taliban bands on Afghan targets also appeared around that time.

As the summer continued attacks in the Taliban heartland increased in frequency. Dozens of Afghan government soldiers, non-governmental organization and humanitarian workers and several U.S. soldiers died in the raids, ambushes and rocket attacks. In addition to the guerrilla attacks, Taliban fighters began building up their forces in the district of Dai Chopan, a district in Zabul Province that also straddles Kandahar and Uruzgan that is at the very centre of the Taliban heartland. Dai Chopan district is a remote and sparsely populated corner of southeastern Afghanistan composed of towering, rocky, mountains

The First Casualty

interspersed with narrow gorges. Taliban fighters decided it would be the perfect area to make a stand against the Afghan government and the coalition forces. Over the course of the summer, perhaps the largest concentration of Taliban militants gathered in the area since the fall of the regime, with up to 1,000 guerrillas regrouping. Over 220 people, including several dozen Afghan police, were killed in August 2003 as Taliban fighters gained strength.

As a result, coalition forces began preparing offensives to root out the rebel forces. In late August 2005, Afghan government forces backed by U.S troops and heavy American aerial bombardment advanced upon Taliban positions within the mountain fortress. After a one-week battle Taliban forces were routed with up to 124 fighters (according to Afghan government estimates) killed. Taliban spokesmen, however, denied the high casualty figure and U.S estimates were somewhat lower.

◇

From January 2006, a NATO International Security Assistance Force (ISAF) started to replace the U.S. troops of Operation Enduring Freedom in southern Afghanistan. The British 16th Air Assault Brigade (later reinforced by Royal Marines) formed the core of the force in Southern Afghanistan, along with troops and helicopters from Australia, Canada and the Netherlands. The initial force consisted of roughly 3,300 British, 2,300 Canadian, 1,963 from the Netherlands, 290 from Denmark, 300 from

Australia, and 150 from Estonia. Air support was provided by U.S., British, Dutch, Norwegian and French combat aircraft and helicopters.

In January 2006 NATO's focus in southern Afghanistan was to form Provincial Reconstruction Teams with the British leading in Helmand Province and, the Netherlands and Canada would lead similar deployments in Orūzgān Province and Kandahar Province respectively. Local Taliban figures voiced opposition to the incoming force and pledged to resist it.

Southern Afghanistan faced in 2006 the deadliest spate of violence in the country since the ousting of the Taliban regime by U.S-led forces in 2001, as the newly deployed NATO troops battled resurgent militants. NATO operations have been led by British, Canadian and Dutch commanders. Operation Mountain Thrust was launched on May 17, 2006 with the purpose of rooting out Taliban forces. In July, Canadian Forces launched Operation Medusa in an attempt to clear the areas of Taliban fighters once and for all, supported by U.S., British, Dutch and Danish forces. Further NATO operations included the Battle of Panjwaii, Operation Mountain Fury and Operation Falcon Summit. The fighting for NATO forces was intense throughout the second half of 2006. NATO has been successful in achieving tactical victories over the Taliban and denied areas to them but, the Taliban were not completely defeated and NATO had to continue operations into 2007.

The First Casualty

In January and February 2007, British Royal Marines mounted *Operation Volcano* to clear insurgents from firing points in the village of Barikju, north of Kajaki. This was followed by *Operation Achilles*, a major offensive that started in March and ended in late May. The UK Ministry of Defence announced its intention to bring British troop levels in the country up to 7,700 (committed until 2009). Further operations, such as *Operation Silver* and *Operation Silicon*, were conducted to keep up the pressure on the Taliban in the hopes of blunting their expected spring offensive.

On 4 March 2007, at least 12 civilians were killed and 33 were injured by U.S. Marines in the Shinwar district of the Nangrahar province of Afghanistan as the Americans reacted to a bomb ambush. The event has become known in the district as the Shinwar Massacre, and was considered a propaganda coup for the Taliban. The 120 member Marine unit responsible for the attack was asked to leave the country because the incident damaged the unit's relations with the local Afghan population.

On 12 May 2007 ISAF forces killed Mullah Dadullah, Taliban commander in charge of leading operations in the south of the country; eleven other Taliban fighters were killed in the same fire fight. This was a great success for the coalition, not only in terms of removing a major commander from the field but also in terms of propaganda success.

The First Casualty

During the summer, NATO forces achieved tactical victories over the Taliban at the Battle of Chora in Orūzgān Province, where Dutch and Australian ISAF forces are deployed. On August 28, 2007, at least 100 Taliban fighters and one Afghan National Army soldier were killed in several skirmishes in the Shah Wali Kot district of Kandahar province.

On 28 October 2007 about 80 Taliban fighters were killed in a 24hour battle with forces from the U.S-led coalition in Afghanistan's Helmand province.

During the last days of October, Canadian forces surrounded around 300 militants near Arghandab and killed at least 50 of them. This was said to have stopped a potential Taliban offensive on Kandahar.

Taliban losses were mounting. Yet it did not appear to blunt their effectiveness. The strength of Taliban forces was estimated by Western officials and analysts at about 10,000 fighters fielded at any given time, according to a report on 30 October in *The New York Times*. Of that number, 'only 2,000 to 3,000 are highly motivated, full-time insurgents', the *Times* reported. The rest are part-timers, made up of alienated, young Afghan men angry at bombing raids or fighting in order to earn money.

In 2007 more foreign fighters were showing up in Afghanistan than ever before, according to Afghan and

The First Casualty

United States officials. An estimated 100 to 300 full-time combatants are foreigners, usually from Pakistan, Uzbekistan, Chechnya, various Arab countries and perhaps even Turkey and western China. They tend to be more fanatical and violent and they often bring skills such as the ability to post more sophisticated videos on the Internet, as well as bomb making expertise. The losses of Coalition troops, killed or wounded, by roadside bombs have done much to turn public opinion in Western countries, not least in the United Kingdom, against involvement in the war.

On 2 November 2007 Afghan security forces killed a top-ranking militant, Mawlawi Abdul Manan, after he was caught trying to cross into Afghanistan from neighbouring Pakistan. The Taliban confirmed his death.

Eight days later, on 10 November 2007, the Taliban ambushed a patrol in eastern Afghanistan killing six American and three Afghan soldiers whilst losing only one insurgent. This attack brought the U.S. death toll for 2007 to 100, making it the deadliest year for Americans in Afghanistan.

Security operations were conducted in the north by ISAF and Afghan forces, including Operation Harekate Yolo I & II. Norwegian and German soldiers took part in the operation. The exact death toll was not disclosed at the time but, according to Norwegian news reports, 'between 20 and 25 insurgents' were killed in action, while the German Ministry of Defence verified a further 14 hostile fighters killed in action. The operation ended on 6 November 2007.

The Battle of Musa Qala took place in December 2007. Afghan units were the principal fighting force supported by British forces. Taliban forces were forced to pull out of Musa Qala.

◇

On 27 April, President Karzai escaped another attempt on his life: gunmen opened fire during a military parade celebrating the nation's victory and liberation from the eight year occupation of the Soviet Union. The fire fight lasted about a quarter of an hour with three dead and about a dozen wounded.

On 29 April, 2,300 U.S Marines attacked the town of Garmsir in Helmand province, a region of Afghanistan where the Taliban had a stronghold. It was at this time that the numbers of American combatants increased in number. In the first 5 months of 2008 the number of U.S. troops in Afghanistan increased by over 80% with a surge of 21,643 more troops, bringing the total number of U.S. troops in Afghanistan from 26,607 in January to 48,250 in June. In September 2008 George Bush announced the withdrawal of over 8,000 troops from Iraq in the coming months and a further increase of up to 4,500 U.S. troops in Afghanistan.

In May, Norwegian-led ISAF forces conducted a military

operation in Badghis province.

In June British Prime Minster Gordon Brown announced the number of British troops serving in Afghanistan would increase to 8,030 - a rise of 230 personnel. That same month the UK lost its 100th serviceman killed in the war since 2001.

On 13 June Taliban fighters demonstrated their ongoing strength, liberating all prisoners in Kandahar jail. The well-planned operation freed 1200 prisoners, 400 of whom were Taliban prisoners-of-war, causing a major embarrassment for NATO in one of its operational centres in the country.

On 13 July 2008 a coordinated Taliban attack was launched on a remote NATO base at Wanat in the Kunar province. On 19 August French troops suffered their worse losses in Afghanistan in an ambush. Later in the month an air strike, that targeted a Taliban commander in Herat province, killed 90 civilians.

Late August saw one of the largest operations by NATO forces in Helmand province, *Operation Eagle's Summit*, with the aim of bringing electricity to the region. You might not be able to win hearts and minds but you could ensure they had electrical supplies.

On 3 September the war spilled over on to Pakistani territory for the first time when heavily armed

The First Casualty

commandos, believed to be US Special Forces, landed by helicopter and attacked three houses in a village close to a known Taliban and Al-Qaeda stronghold. The attack killed between seven and twenty people. According to local residents most of the dead were civilians. Pakistan responded furiously condemning the attack. The foreign ministry in Islamabad called the incursion a gross violation of Pakistan's territory'.

On 6 September, in an apparent reaction to the recent cross-border attack, the federal government announced disconnection of supply lines to the allied forces stationed in Afghanistan through Pakistan for an indefinite period.

On 11 September militants killed two U.S. troops in the eastern part of the country. This brought the total number of US losses to 113, making 2008 the deadliest year for American troops in Afghanistan since the start of the war. The year was also the deadliest for several European countries with soldiers fighting in Afghanistan.

By January 2009 the Taliban was making the exaggerated claim that they had killed 5,220 foreign troops, downed 31 aircraft, destroyed 2,818 NATO and Afghan vehicles and killed 7,552 Afghan soldiers and police in 2008 alone. The Associated Press estimated that a total of 286 foreign military personnel were actually killed in Afghanistan in 2008.

The Khyber Border Coordination Centre between the U.S.,

The First Casualty

Pakistan, and Afghanistan, at Torkham on the Afghan side of the Khyber Pass, has been in operation for nine months. It has not been a success. Language barriers have been a problem. It often comes as a surprise to both American and British that not all the world speaks their language fluently or at all. Border disputes between Pakistani and Afghan field officers do not help either and long-standing mistrust among all three militaries has hampered progress.

In January, about 3,000 U.S. soldiers from the 3rd Brigade Combat Team of the 10th Mountain Division moved into the provinces of Logar and Wardak. The troops were the first wave of an expected surge of reinforcements originally ordered by George W. Bush and increased by Barack Obama. In mid-February it was announced that 17,000 additional troops would be deployed to the country in two brigades and additional support troops; the 2nd Marine Expeditionary Brigade of about 3,500 from the 7,000 Marines and the 5th Brigade, 2nd Infantry Division, a Stryker Brigade with about 4,000 of the 7,000 US Army soldiers. The U.S. commander in Afghanistan, General McKiernan, had called for as many as 30,000 additional troops, effectively doubling the number of troops currently in the country.

There were, during November and December 2008, multiple incidents of major theft, robbery, and arson attacks against NATO supply convoys in Pakistan. Transport companies south of Kabul have also been reported to pay protection money to the Taliban. In an

The First Casualty

attack on 11 November, 2008 Taliban fighters in Peshawar hijacked a convoy carrying NATO supplies from Karachi to Afghanistan. The militants took two military Humvees and paraded them in front of the media as trophies.

The coalition forces bring 70 per cent of supplies through Pakistan every month, a total of 2,000 truckloads in all.

The area east of the Khyber Pass in Pakistan has seen frequent attacks. Cargo trucks and Humvees have been set ablaze by Taliban militants. Half a dozen raids on depots with NATO supplies near Peshawar destroyed 300 cargo trucks and Humvees in December 2008. The Taliban destroyed an iron bridge on the highway between Peshawar and the Khyber Pass in February 2009.

On Dec 30, 2008 Pakistani security forces shut down the supply line when they launched an offensive against Taliban militants who dominate the Khyber Pass region. After three days of fighting they declared the Khyber Pass open.

The other supply route through Pakistan, via Chaman, was briefly shut down in early 2009. On Jan 10 tribesmen used vehicles to block the road to protest a raid by Pakistani counter-narcotics forces that left one villager dead. The protesters withdrew on Jan 14 after police promised to take their complaints to provincial authorities.

In response to the increased risk of sending supplies

The First Casualty

through Pakistan work began on the establishment of a Northern Distribution Network (NDN) through Russia and several Central Asian republics. Initial permission for the U.S military to move troop supplies through the region was given on 20 January 2009 after a visit to the region by General Petraeus. Though U.S. forces were evicted from Manas Air Base in Kyrgyzstan only a few days later, on February 3, transit agreements between the U.S. and Kyrgyzstan, as well as the other Central Asian republics, remained in effect. The first shipment along the NDN route left on February 20 from Riga, Latvia then travelled 3,212 miles (5,169 km) to the Uzbekistan town of Termez on the Afghanistan border. U.S. commanders have stated their hope that 100 containers a day will be shipped along the NDN. By comparison currently 140 containers a day are shipped through the Khyber Pass.

On May 11, 2009 Uzbekistan president Islam Karimov announced that the airport in Navoi, Uzbekistan was being used to transport non-lethal cargo into Afghanistan. Due to the still unsettled relationship between Uzbekistan and the United States following the 2005 Andijon massacre and subsequent expulsion of U.S. forces from Karshi-Khanabad airbase, U.S. forces were not involved in the shipment of supplies. Instead South Korea's Korean Air, which is currently involved in overhauling Navoi's airport, officially handles logistics at the site.

Some analysts worry that use of the NDN will come at the cost of increased Russian demands concerning missile defence and NATO enlargement. Additionally, human rights advocates are concerned that the U.S. is again working with the government of Uzbekistan, which is often accused of violating human rights. Nevertheless, U.S. officials have promised increased cooperation with Uzbekistan, including further assistance to turn the Navoi airport into a major regional distribution centre for both military and civilian ventures

An unnamed senior Pentagon official told the BBC that at some point between 12 July and 12 September 2008 President George W. Bush issued a classified order to authorize U.S. raids against militants in Pakistan. Pakistan, however, said it would not allow foreign forces onto its territory and that it would vigorously protect its sovereignty. In September, the Pakistan military stated that it had issued orders to open fire on American soldiers who crossed the Pakistan border in pursuit of militant forces.

On 25 September 2008 Pakistani troops shot towards ISAF helicopters that belonged to American troops. This caused confusion and anger in the Pentagon who asked for a full explanation into the incident and denied that American choppers were in Pakistani airspace. Pakistan's President Asif Ali Zardari was quick to deny that shots were fired but, instead insisted that the Pakistani troops shot flares to warn the Americans that they were in Pakistani airspace. This added to the doubts that were expressed by certain Pentagon and Bush Administration officials about the capabilities of the Pakistani Armed

The First Casualty

Forces to confront the militant threat. This has all added to the split that occurred when American troops apparently landed on Pakistani soil to carry out an operation against militants in the North-West Frontier Province but, 'Pakistan reacted angrily to the action, saying 20 innocent villagers had been killed by US troops'.

On 1 October 2008 a suspected U.S drone fired a missile against militants inside Pakistan's North-West Frontier Province near the Afghan border. It is believed that six people died in the incident. Such attacks and they have not ceased, have drawn a stiff response from Islamabad, accusing the United States of violating their airspace. Although Americans have expressed frustration at the lack or failure of action by the Pakistani side against the militants holed up on Pakistani soil.

In November 2006 the U.N. Security Council warned that Afghanistan may become a failed state because of increased Taliban violence, growing illegal drug production and fragile State institutions. In 2006, Afghanistan was rated 10th on the failed states index, up from 11th in 2005. The central government had little power and control beyond the capital city of Kabul. From 2005 to 2006 the number of suicide attacks, direct fire attacks and improvised explosive devices all increased. Intelligence documents declassified in 2006 suggested that Al-Qaeda, Taliban, Haqqani Network and Hezb-i-Islami sanctuaries had increased fourfold in Afghanistan. The campaign in Afghanistan successfully unseated the Taliban from power, but has been significantly less successful at achieving the primary policy goal of ensuring that Al-Qaeda can no longer operate in Afghanistan.

BBC News released an article on June 19, 2007 about life in Afghanistan since the U.S. occupation. The article focuses on the life of the villagers of Asad Khyl. What seems to be suggested is that security in Afghanistan is better but poverty and corruption remain a major problem.

General David H. Petraeus, former head of U.S. troops in Iraq who was transferred to be head of Central Command, admitted that the Taliban were gaining in strength. He cited the recent increase in attacks in Afghanistan and in neighbouring Pakistan. Petraeus also insisted that the challenges faced in Afghanistan were more complicated than the ones that were faced in Iraq during his tour. He concluded that in order to turn around the situation there was a need to remove militant sanctuaries and strongholds that were widespread inside Afghanistan.

On 1 October 2008 the top American general in Afghanistan, David McKiernan, warned that the situation in Afghanistan could get a lot worse. The international forces within Afghanistan have not been able to hold territory they have cleared because of the lack of troops. For this reason the general called for an extra three combat brigades (roughly 20,000 troops). Without this urgent rush of troops the Taliban would be able to get back into the communities that were once cleared by international troops. Generals always ask for more troops, as if that were always the solution to a problem.

The problem is compounded, too, by a lack of agreement on objectives in the war, a lack of resources, lack of coordination and too great a focus on the weak and corrupt central government at the expense of local and provincial governments. Indeed, there is a developing appreciation that concentration needs to be on the region and not merely on Afghanistan. What American and NATO politicians and generals have further admitted is that the war is not going to be a short one. Decades are being mentioned. The Allies are digging in and in particular thousands of U.S. troops in Afghanistan are stationed in large, permanent bases.

In February 2005, U.S. Senator John McCain – candidate for the American presidency against Barack Obama in 2008, called for the establishment of permanent U.S. military bases in Afghanistan, saying such bases would be 'for the good of the American people, because of the long-term security interests we have in the region.' McCain did not win the White House but his view is generally accepted. He made the remarks whilst visiting Afghan President Hamid Karzai in Kabul as part of a five-member, bi-partisan Senate delegation travelling through the region for talks on security issues. The same delegation included then Senator Hillary Clinton, now U.S. Secretary of State.

The First Casualty

In mid-March, 2005, U.S. Joint Chiefs of Staff Chairman General Richard Myers told reporters in Kabul that the U.S. Defence Department was studying the feasibility of such permanent military bases. At the end of March, the U.S. military announced that it was spending $83-million on its two main air bases in Afghanistan, Bagram Air Base north of Kabul and Kandahar Air Field in the south of the country.

A few weeks after this series of U.S. statements, in April 2005, during a surprise visit to Kabul by U.S. Defence Secretary Donald Rumsfeld, Afghan President Hamid Karzai hinted at a possible permanent U.S. military presence in Afghanistan, saying he had also discussed the matter with President Bush. Rumsfeld refused to say whether or not the U.S. wanted permanent American military bases in Afghanistan, saying the final decision would come from the White House.

As of July 2008, hundreds of millions of dollars were being spent on permanent infrastructure for foreign military bases in Afghanistan, including a budget of $780-million to further develop the infrastructure at just the Kandahar Air Field base; described as 'a walled, multicultural military city that houses some 13,000 troops from 17 different countries - the kind of place where you can eat at a Dutch chain restaurant alongside soldiers from the Royal Netherlands Army.' The Bagram Air Base, run by the U.S. military, was also expanding, with the U.S military buying land from Afghan locals in different places

The First Casualty

for further expansion of the base.

As of January 2009 the U.S. had begun work on $1.6 billion worth of new, permanent military installations. In February 2009, *The Times* of London repeated the story, stating that the United States intends to build new military bases in southern Afghanistan. One will be built in Kandahar province near the Helmand border, at Maiwand - a place famous as the site of the destruction of a British army during the Second Anglo-Afghan War. The other new U.S. military base will be built in Zabul, a province now largely controlled by the Taliban. The Allies are in Afghanistan for the long haul. And not everyone has been heartened by this dramatic build-up of an indefinite Western military presence. The government of Russia, strenuously seeking to regain its place at the top table of important nations, has expressed disapproval. 'Is it all to fight a number of Taliban - 10,000, 12,000 Taliban?' Zamir Kabulov, Russia's ambassador to Kabul has questioned. 'Maybe this infrastructure, military infrastructure, [is] not only for internal purposes but for regional also.' This hits the nail on the head. Russia views the large and indefinite military build-up as a potential threat because – and we are now back to Sir Halford Mackinder - Afghanistan's geographical location is a very strategic one, being close to the three main world basins of hydrocarbons: the Persian Gulf, Caspian Sea, and Central Asia. Other observers have also noted that through a stronger military presence in Afghanistan, the U.S. may be seeking to strengthen its own position in the region to counter

The First Casualty

increasingly warm relations between India, Russia and China. And, of course, Afghanistan is a neighbour of Iran, still a main player in the region, as it has been ever since the time of Alexander the Great. The United States long ago entered the Great Game, the greatest game of all in the world, and, indeed, the only game of any significance. Except that to use the term *game* is to diminish the stature of all who are risking their lives and livelihoods daily.

The International Security Assistance Force (ISAF) is an international stabilization force authorized by the United Nations Security Council on December 20, 2001. On July 31, 2006 the NATO-led International Security Assistance Force assumed command of the south of the country and by 5 October 2006 also of the east part of Afghanistan. By mid 2009, ISAF numbers were: 58,390, of which more than 26,000 are Americans and eight and a half thousand are British troops.

◇

Although the war was initially supported by most of America, the UN Security Council and NATO, many people in the world, Europeans in particular, now oppose the war. In a 47-nation June 2007 survey of global public opinion, there was considerable opposition to U.S. and NATO operations in Afghanistan. Only in just four out of the 47 countries surveyed was there a majority that favoured keeping foreign troops: the U.S. (50%), Israel (59%), Ghana (50%), and Kenya (60%). In 41 of the 47 countries, pluralities want U.S. and NATO troops out of Afghanistan as soon as possible. The opinions of the populace rarely count for much. People are swayed by newspaper articles, television programmes, and generally know little, if anything, of the situation on the ground, and even less of the political and strategic issues involved. However, in fairness, it has to be said that since the June 2008 global survey, public opinion in Australia and Britain has also diverged from that in the U.S., and a majority of Australians and Britons now want their troops to be brought home from Afghanistan. A September 2008 poll found that 56% of Australians oppose the continuation of their country's military involvement in Afghanistan, while 42% support it. A November 2008 poll found that 68% of Britons want their troops withdrawn within the next 12 months. In the United States, a September 2008 Pew survey found that 61% of Americans wanted U.S. troops to stay until the situation has stabilized, while 33% wanted them removed as soon as possible.

Public opinion at the beginning of the war also reflected this dichotomy between the United States and most other countries. When the invasion began in October 2001, polls indicated that about 88% of Americans and about 65% of Britons supported military action in Afghanistan. On the other hand, a large-scale 37-nation poll of world opinion carried out by Gallup International in late September 2001, found that large majorities in most countries favoured a legal response, in the form of extradition and trial, over a military response to 9/11: Only in just 3

The First Casualty

countries out of the 37 surveyed - the United States, Israel, and India - did majorities favour military action in Afghanistan. In 34 out of the 37 countries surveyed, the survey found many clear and sizeable majorities that did not favour military action: in the United Kingdom (75%), France (67%), Switzerland (87%), Czech Republic (64%), Lithuania (83%), Panama (80%), Mexico (94%) and other countries. However, since the Taliban refused to hand over bin Laden or his followers for trial, extradition was not a viable option by the time the war began. An Ipsos-Reid poll conducted between November and December 2001 showed that majorities in Canada (66%), France (60%), Germany (60%), Italy (58%) and the U.K. (65%) approved of U.S. air strikes while majorities in Argentina (77%), China (52%), South Korea (50%), Spain (52%) and Turkey (70%) opposed them.

Polls are rarely valuable and opinions tend to be based on emotional rather than rational responses. The war has repeatedly been the subject of protests around the world starting with the large-scale demonstrations in the days leading up to the official launch of U.S. Operation Enduring Freedom under George W. Bush in October 2001 and every year since. Protesters consider the bombing and invasion of Afghanistan to be unjustified aggression. The deaths of thousands of Afghan civilians caused directly and indirectly by the U.S. and NATO bombing campaigns is also a major underlying focus of the protests. These people are often naïve liberals who will join any protest that affords shouting in the streets. There may well be legitimate concerns – there are – but rent-a-crowd liberals know little of these.

Regarding civilian casualties of the War in Afghanistan from 2001 to the present day, there are no reliable figures and, given the nature of the conflict, there probably never will be. In time of war both or all sides commit atrocities. That is human nature when it is in extreme situations and individuals lose whatever moral compass they had in the first place. We need also to remember that individuals who would not commit an atrocity will often do so when they become part of a group, especially a group without proper central control, or with leaders who are prepared to countenance extreme behaviour. A mob or a herd is not merely a group of individuals; there is something added. One has only to observe the behaviour of people at football matches to understand that individuals within a herd are not reasonable.

The UN Assistance Mission in Afghanistan (UNAMA) has reported that in the year 2008 alone more than two thousand Afghan civilians were killed by armed conflict, this being the highest figure since the beginning of the invasion. Some have claimed that the figure is double this, and perhaps even higher than five thousand, but evidence is hard to attain. While not all civilian casualties are inflicted by air strikes, it is probably correct to say that air strikes on villages and towns are responsible for high civilian death rates and casualties. There was a tacit admission of this when, in March 2009, General

The First Casualty

McChrystal announced new restrictions on air strikes in order to reduce civilian casualties. Whether this was to appease a restless electorate and mere window dressing, it is impossible to know. What is certain is that air strikes continue but the emphasis now seems to be hitting insurgents in the border areas with Pakistan. In any case, in such a war as this one, a fighter by night can become a peasant tilling is fields by day; a committed soldier will break ranks when it is time to return home to harvest the poppy seeds.

War is hell. Anyone who says different does not understand war. Yet a strange phenomenon has developed of late. In both the USA and Britain there has grown up a group of civilians who think that wars can be conducted without civilian casualties. They go further too: they believe wars can be fought without military casualties. As soon as coffins start to be unloaded from transport planes – seen clearly on television screens – there is a public demand in newspaper letters columns and on phone-in radio programmes, for the country to withdraw from the war. Naïve is too weak a word to describe such people. One does not need to be a pacifist or a supporter of this conflict to know that in war there are certain to be casualties.

David Miliband, Foreign Secretary in the government of the United Kingdom, in an article in the *Daily Telegraph* newspaper, on 17 August 2009, strongly defended the role of British troops in Afghanistan, in the face of mounting

The First Casualty

criticism over the number of military casualties. The figure of military deaths had reached 204, 'a reminder of the bravery of our soldiers and the sacrifices they make every day.' It was, he said, understandable that people were asking questions: why the British were in Afghanistan and for how long. People also wanted to know how long the conflict would continue and whether the loss of life was justified. The Coalition was in Afghanistan through necessity. As the home of international terrorism, the border region of Afghanistan and Pakistan remained the primary threat to Britain's national security. Having driven Al-Qaeda out of Afghanistan, they must not be allowed to return 'under the safe umbrella of Taliban rule.' British soldiers were fighting in a coalition of 42 allies, and alongside Afghan government forces, to push the Taliban out of the towns and villages and ensure they stay out.

One source of the Taliban's strength, but also its vulnerability, is that they are an amalgam of different groups – a coalition of convenience. They recruit foot soldiers at $10 a day. Narco-traffickers work with them to get safe passage for drugs. Warlords, believing the Taliban will win, position themselves for their own political advantage. Perhaps most crucially, Afghans, despite dreading the Taliban's return, fear that international forces will leave before the Afghan state is ready to protect them.

So, Miliband said, they hedge their bets. For many people - indeed for everyone - the name of the game is survival. 'Whether military breakthroughs are translated into strategic success depends on politics – crucially the ability of the political system to incorporate people currently acquiescent to or supportive of violence. International and Afghan forces can keep the insurgents on the back foot. But only legitimate, clean and competent Afghan government, recognising local tribal structures as well as national democratic ones, can provide an alternative focus for loyalty. Effective protection and a better life is the best way to keep the insurgency at bay.' Yet a General Election roused little interest, and there was well-founded evidence of corruption, intimidation and vote rigging by the Karzai government in Kabul. This same Afghan government, deeply corrupt, must – Miliband continued - deepen cooperation with its neighbours, particularly Pakistan. The Pakistani military offensive launched in April meant that for the first time the insurgency was being squeezed on both sides of the border. Fine words from an intelligent politician intended for his own electorate. These words did not, however, state the truth of the situation. Yet they came close. The mention of Pakistan is significant. The Coalition cannot afford to allow Pakistan to fall to the Taliban, Al-Qaeda jihadists, Islamist extremists – the names are almost interchangeable – because Pakistan is a nation with stocks of nuclear weapons. Al-Qaeda with the bomb is a nightmare scenario, making the attack on the Twin Towers in New York, with the loss of three thousand civilian lives, look like a mild altercation at a tea party held at a local vicarage. Al-Qaeda in possession of the Bomb has been described as Existential Horror.

The First Casualty

It is not necessary to be a defender of the Taliban – and we are certainly not that – to accept that not everything done during Taliban government in Afghanistan was unacceptable. In 2000, the Taliban issued a ban on opium production, which led to reductions in Pashtun Mafia opium production by as much as 90%. Soon after the 2001 U.S. led invasion of Afghanistan opium production increased markedly. By 2005, Afghanistan had regained its position as the world's leading producer of opium, producing 90% of the world's opium, most of which is processed into heroin and sold in Europe and Russia. While U.S. and allied efforts to combat the drug trade have been stepped up, the effort is hampered by the fact that many suspected drug traffickers are now leading officials in the Karzai government. Recent estimates by the United Nations Office on Drugs and Crime (UNODC) estimate that 52% of the nation's GDP, amounting to $2.7 billion annually, is generated by the drug trade. The rise in production has been linked to the deteriorating security situation, as production is markedly lower in areas with stable security. The poppy eradication policy propagated by the international community, in particular the United States, as part of their War on Drugs, has been a failure, exacerbated by the lack of alternative development projects to replace livelihoods lost as a result of poppy eradication. Seeking to eradicate poppy cultivation the Allies have succeeded only in increasing poverty in rural areas. Poppy eradication has succeeded only in adding to the extreme poverty in rural areas, not least in the south of Afghanistan. The extermination of the poppy crops is not seen as a viable option, due to the fact that the sale of poppies constitute the livelihood of Afghanistan's rural farmers. Opium is more profitable than wheat and destroying opium fields leads to discontent and unrest amongst the population. Alternatives to poppy eradication have so far failed.

◇

We hear a great deal these days about human rights. If truth is the first casualty of war, perhaps human rights are the second. This is not something that has arisen from the invasion in 2001. Afghanistan has suffered extensive human rights violations over the last twenty years. When armed factions struggle to achieve supremacy, there are going to be abuses. War is not a game for gentlemen, and especially not civil conflict. The Taliban rose to power in 1998 and ruled Afghanistan for five years, during which years they became notorious for their human rights abuses against women.

According to Amnesty International – a group that zealously seeks to find the truth in a situation and report it accurately, without fear and without favour to any government or group - the Taliban commit war crimes by targeting civilians, including killing teachers, abducting aid workers and burning school buildings. Amnesty International claims that up to 756 civilians were killed in 2006 by bombs, mostly on roads or carried by suicide attackers belonging to the Taliban.

The First Casualty

In addition, Afghan warlords and political strongmen have been responsible for numerous human rights violations including kidnapping, rape, robbery, and extortion. This is no land for the timid or the squeamish.

It has been claimed that top officials at the CIA authorized controversial, harsh interrogation techniques. The Bush administration declared that Al-Qaeda members captured on the battlefield were not subject to the Geneva Conventions as this was not a conventional war. Amnesty International stated in 2007 that an agreement to allow Canadian officials to visit enemy detainees in Afghanistan was aimed more at saving political face than keeping prisoners safe. Interrogation techniques included shaking and slapping, shackling prisoners in a standing position, keeping the prisoner in a cold cell and dousing them with water and most controversially of all water boarding.

Water boarding is not new, although the name may be. It is a form of torture that consists of immobilizing the victim on his or her back with the head inclined downwards. Water is poured over the face and into the breathing passages. By forced suffocation and inhalation of water, the subject experiences the sensation of drowning.

Water boarding precipitates an almost immediate gag reflex. The technique does not inevitably cause lasting physical damage. It can, however, cause extreme pain, dry drowning, damage to lungs, brain damage from oxygen

The First Casualty

deprivation, and other physical injuries including broken bones due to struggling against restraints, lasting psychological damage or, if uninterrupted, death. This is not a new technique. The torturer's art is ancient and has many variations.

In 2007 it was reported that the Central Intelligence Agency (CIA) was using water boarding on extra-judicial prisoners and that the United States Department of Justice had authorized that boarding was sanctioned by the Bush administration. In January 2009, in one of the first acts of his presidency, Barack Obama banned the use of water boarding.

The Allies have alleged that the Taliban have used indefensible tactics too. It is alleged that Taliban uses civilians as human shields. NATO has pointed to the victims of air strikes in Farah province in May 2009 in which the Afghan government claimed up to 150 civilians were killed. NATO stated that it had evidence that the Taliban forced civilians into buildings likely to be targeted by NATO aircraft involved in the battle. US Lieutenant Colonel Greg Julian, a spokesman for NATO's Afghanistan commander, said of the Taliban's tactics, 'This was a deliberate plan by the Taliban to create a civilian casualty crisis. These were not human shields; these were human sacrifices. We have intelligence that points to this. Patient after patient just kept telling the doctors their story and how they were forced by the Taliban to stay in these locations.'

The First Casualty

There is little point in further cataloguing abuses by all parties in this conflict. War is hell and it could be argued that in such a situation it is foolish to promulgate rules of conduct. The important thing is not to sling mud, to allege this and that, but to consider how the conflict may be terminated.

◇

The First World War lasted four years and World War II lasted six years. The Afghanistan War looks to be of much longer duration. The current Allied commander in Afghanistan, American General Stanley McChrystal asserted that troop deaths are a price worth paying. This was a response to criticisms, especially in NATO countries, that casualties were becoming too high and that the invasion had proved unnecessary. McChrystal stated that despite some progress being made many indicators point to a general deterioration in the overall state of Afghanistan. If the government were to fall to the Taliban, he said, Afghanistan could again become a base for terrorism. 'We face not only a resilient and growing insurgency; there is also a crisis of confidence among Afghans - in both their government and the international community - that undermines our credibility and emboldens the insurgents.' General McChrystal's suggested remedy was an increase in resources, both military and civilian. He says that he needs a 'jump' in resources, both civilian and military to defeat the insurgency. Additional resources alone would not win the war, but under-resourcing, as he put it, could lose the war.

In addition, McChrystal said, a new strategy was needed. It was vital to win the support of the Afghan population. This is another way of saying that the Allies must win the hearts and minds of the people being invaded. This, we submit, is not likely to be successful. The Allies are foreign troops and as memories of Taliban puritanism fade, it is likely that many Afghans will choose their own people over foreigners. Those that do not revert to supporting the Taliban are likely to side with the many warlords. 'Additional resources are required,' said the General, 'but focusing on force or resource requirements misses the point entirely. The key take away from this assessment is the urgent need for a significant change to our strategy and the way that we think and operate.' The war, he stated – and this view has been echoed by British generals – is going to take decades rather than years. It is important to convince the Afghan people that there is a resolve to win the war against the Taliban and they need not fear giving their support.

General McChrystal also referred to the size of the Afghan national army. Its present strength is about 92,000 men. It needs to be increased to 240,000. The police force needs to grow from 84,000 police to 160,000. Possibly as a nod to liberal opinion in the United States and in NATO countries, McChrystal says that all detention centres, including the prison at Bagram Air Base, are to be

The First Casualty

eventually handed over to the Afghan authorities when they have the capacity to run them. If he believes that this will improve the situation in prisons in Afghanistan he is deluding himself.

◇

So can the West win the war in Afghanistan? If the history of foreign invasions into Afghanistan is anything to go by the answer must be in the negative. The British, at their height of power in Victorian times, could not hold the country and in more recent times the Soviets suffered a crushing defeat after a decade of waste of armour and manpower. Now the Americans have joined the Great Game – which is not a game at all, but a deadly and brutal series of battles, renewed strategies, troop surges; and for what?

This is the question that is being asked everywhere in the West. Why are we in Afghanistan? Why are lives being lost? When will withdrawal begin? And what many people dare not ask is what would be the result if the West were to withdraw?

After what seemed a relatively easy initial victory the Taliban is again resurgent. Now the West appears to be repeating all the mistakes made by the Soviets. The Soviet hierarchy believed that they could use a small number of Marxists to create a compliant satellite in the very heartland. They were wrong. With American assistance to

The First Casualty

the mujahideen there was strong resistance to the invader. Afghanistan is a Muslim country and Islam has not accepted the tenets of Marxism, especially one imposed by a foreign army. The Soviets had to withdraw and there was popular support for the withdrawal in Russia.

Thus, when the USA defeated the Taliban it needed only three hundred American Special Forces to assist the Afghans. Then the Americans started to make some of the mistakes made earlier by the Soviets. There was initial goodwill in many parts of Afghanistan; people were pleased to see the back of the repressive Taliban regime. What, perhaps, was needed - and this is the opinion of some critics - was to build up the government and economic structures of the country and then get out swiftly. But instead of such a strategy, the USA is dedicated to the imposition of a modern democratic country. Democracy is as alien to the vast majority of Afghans as is Marxism. The USA, it seems, is duplicating the errors of the Soviets and will perhaps pay the same price in terms of ill will, loss of material, loss of lives. We cannot try to create a modern, centralized, democratic state in Afghanistan from the top down using foreign troops - from forty-one countries remember - to impose Western-style democracy. By Western standards elections are fraudulent and ridden with corruption. For many people, Hamid Karzai, titular President of his country is little more than the Mayor of Kabul. American intelligence sources have admitted, in muted voice perhaps, that Karzai's government is corrupt and that large swathes of territory are once again falling under Taliban control. In part, the resurgence of the Taliban has been due to its cowing of the people, but there is also the view, recognised throughout the ages, that people will support their own kind against foreigners, no matter what are the good intentions of those foreigners.

◇

So what about Pakistan? This is the great conundrum and there are no easy answers. Certainly we have no easy answers to offer.

Afghanistan has ancient links with Pakistan because of its geographical contiguity and traditional, cultural and linguistic connections. Any development in Afghanistan has since 1947 had direct implication on Pakistani society for one reason or another. After the Soviet defeat the unstable situation in Afghanistan ensured that it became a secure harbour for terrorists and extremists from several parts of the world and not merely from within the sub-continental region. Pakistan has subsequently suffered a great deal. The recent American invasion, the war against terrorism, insurgencies and uprisings in the Federally Administered Tribal Areas (FATA) of Pakistan is solid and substantial evidence of instability within Afghanistan.

Secondly, the ever-increasing role of India in the region has posed serious threats to the security of Pakistan as well as Afghanistan. The government and people of Pakistan &

The First Casualty

Afghanistan need to explore ways and in fact, are taking action, to try to safeguard their vital interests in the region. Questions like why is India throwing so much money into Afghanistan? Why has India more than a dozen of its consulates inside destabilised Afghanistan and all along the Pakistani borders? These types of questions spark doubts in peoples' minds and they must be answered before they become flames that can burn.

Reliable intelligence points to the fact that Taliban and other units operate out of Pakistan. The nature of the uncharted border makes this almost inevitable. In modern times it has become accepted by most countries that if your enemy is attacking you from outside then you have the right to instigate cross-border reprisals. It would appear that Al-Qaeda are no longer operating from Afghanistan. Osama Bin Laden has never been found but rumours persist that he or his supporters operate from Pakistan. The Allies attack such units within Pakistan, often using drone aircraft.

Drones are unmanned aerial vehicles or UAVs and are remotely operated. They are not missiles. They can be directed, retrieved and used again and again. They are usually powered by jet engines. They are useful for sending to remote areas, with a pre-programmed plan and a specific target. As well as attack missions, drones are also used for aerial reconnaissance.

There has been Allied success in using drones to target and

The First Casualty

kill known Al-Qaeda and other militant leaders seeking sanctuary in Pakistan. A missile fired by a U.S. drone killed a top Al-Qaeda operations chief and two other militant commanders in the volatile North Waziristan region of Pakistan in September, 2009. Ilyas Kashmiri was a native Pakistani. Pakistani military and intelligence sources said Kashmiri was killed on 7 September in the Machikhel area of North Waziristan. Two other local militant commanders, Hanifullah Janikhel and Kaleemullah, were also killed. In August, 2009 a drone strike in South Waziristan killed Pakistani Taliban leader Baitullah Mehsud, the country's most-wanted militant. He had been accused of engineering suicide bombings of civilian and military targets. U.S. drone strikes have killed several other prominent Al-Qaeda militants in recent years. These include Abu Hamza Rabia, an Egyptian suspected of heading Al-Qaeda's international operations; senior Al-Qaeda leader Abu Laith al Libi; and Abu Sulayman Jazairi, an Algerian explosives specialist.

The United States' tactic of using drones to attack Al-Qaeda and Taliban militants in Pakistan's tribal areas has been one of the more successful of its operations. It has also been the source of public discord between the Pakistani government and Washington. We say *public* deliberately - although Pakistani leaders publicly condemn the attacks, because they sometimes cause civilian casualties, it is widely believed that they tacitly allow the strikes. In the case of Mehsud's death, Pakistani intelligence helped the U.S. pinpoint his location within

The First Casualty

Waziristan and the Pakistan army has directly confronted militants on its own soil on many occasions. One such incident was the capture in the Swat valley of Sher Mohammed Qasab, a Taliban commander. Qasab was arrested in the Charbagh area of the valley, which militants controlled before the Pakistani military launched a major offensive to drive them out in late April, 2009. Qasab has been accused of personally beheading captured Pakistan soldiers and also of setting fire to a girls schools in Swat. The military said he was captured after he and his sons exchanged gunfire with troops. Three of his sons were killed and a fourth was captured.

Pakistan is in some respects an unstable country. It has in its short history been beset by several military coups and failed coup attempts. Civilian governments have usually been short-lived, ineffective, and corrupt. Since independence in 1947, Pakistan has fought three wars against India, lost East Pakistan (now the independent state of Bangla Desh, though in many ways a client of India) and had the long-running sore of the partition of Kashmir. Pakistan soldiers police a fragile border and strive to avoid or at least dampen down sparks that may at any time produce a fresh conflagration with India. In a country riven with provincial and tribal differences, there is only one group within society that cuts across these deep-seated differences and that is the military. It is not surprising that the periods of greatest stability and progress have been when a military dictator such as Zia ul Haq or Pervez Musharaff has been at the helm. The army

The First Casualty

cuts across tribal divisions; it has the power to mobilise quickly and suppress discord. It is the one force that many Pakistanis trust.

Some Western observers have thereby concluded that what Afghanistan needs is a strong man in Kabul, a military dictator. This may well be true. But if such a dictator were installed by the United States, he would be ineffective and seen as a stooge of the invading foreigners. Karzai is not the man, either. Such a leader would have to come from within. Perhaps even now there is a young colonel in the nascent Afghan army who will one day seize control. Yet could such a man command support and establish control in a country so divided by tribe, by loyalty to the warlords and after half the population has fled to exile? And would the United States government, wedded to its notions of democracy, allow such a leader to emerge and take control?

British and American generals call for more troops to be sent to Afghanistan, as if a surge were the answer. It might be a short-term solution, in that areas of land might well be reclaimed from Taliban control, but it would be short-lived. In the same way, politicians talk glibly of winning the hearts and minds of Afghans within the country. This is nonsense. Foreign invaders may be welcome to begin with, perhaps bringing order out of chaos, but they would soon outstay their initial welcome. Any chance of winning hearts and minds was lost within weeks of this invasion.

The First Casualty

Speaking in London, American army General Stanley A. McChrystal said he opposes strategies that would require fewer troops and focus on fighting Al-Qaeda and the Taliban leadership through drone attacks, air strikes and similar approaches.. Such an approach, which would reduce casualties, is favoured by some Obama administration officials, including Vice President Joe Biden. However, counterinsurgency advocates have said that a narrow war effort would leave the Afghan government unprotected from encroachment by the Taliban or other extremist organizations.

It is this strategy debate that is at the heart of a sweeping review requested by President Obama as the administration grapples with a tainted Afghan presidential election, escalating violence and mounting allied casualties. General McChrystal was a participant at a meeting in Washington. He said, 'A strategy that does not leave Afghanistan in a stable position is probably a short-sighted strategy.' The general's repeated requests for more troops on the ground have been refused, at least until a new broader strategy has been agreed. In his speech to the London-based policy group, McChrystal did not make an explicit plea for more troops, but said that the White House debate was over the goals and objectives of the Afghanistan mission.

General McChrystal spoke in London as the U.S. Senate debated a proposal to demand he testify about the war before lawmakers. Senator John McCain, who lost the

The First Casualty

presidential contest to President Obama, was among those who wanted McChrystal to testify. McChrystal did not testify in open Congressional forum but he has repeated his view that the U.S. and its allies have not provided enough resources for the operations in Afghanistan, blaming the shortfall for a 'serious and deteriorating' situation. The fight, he said, must be redefined. 'The objective is the will of the Afghan people. The war, McChrystal said, was ultimately political. All wars are. 'At the end of the day, we don't win by destroying the Taliban, we don't win by body counts, we don't win by number of successful military raids or attacks,' he said. 'We win when the people decide we win'.

The truth is that there are now generals and politicians on the Allied side who are ready to admit that the war in Afghanistan could possibly be lost. It has long been known that the war could not be won; but the admission that defeat is possible is a new response and one that deserves to be given a serious attention. That is surely why the inclusion of elements of the Taliban in a national government for Afghanistan is being talked about.

Another group of vocal critics suggests why not get out of Afghanistan, save the lives of 'our' soldiers and allow the Afghans to stew in their own divisive juices? So be it if that means the return to Kabul of a Taliban government. So be it if it means brutal reprisals and the settling of scores on a large scale. It would not be the first bloodbath in history but it would be an important one for the twenty-first century.

Having been fed many lies by a discredited Government – weapons of mass destruction, immigration numbers, education standards, the Lisbon Treaty, boom and bust – the people of the United Kingdom are in no mood to trust their government. Pictures of coffins, draped in the Union flag, arriving in England are shown almost daily on national television. People are questioning the reasons for involvement in Afghanistan and questioning the cost in British lives. There are similar stirrings in the United States and, perhaps to a lesser extent, in NATO countries. For no matter how many times Gordon Brown tells the British people that soldiers are dying in Helmand to make safe the streets of London, polls keep showing that a majority rejects his assertion.

Ever since 2006, when John Reid, then Secretary for Defence, offered hope that British troops could be home within three years – an outcome that seemed unlikely even then – the government has been on the wrong side of public opinion. With more than 200 fatalities and scores injured, the price of engagement is one the British voters are reluctant to pay. There is less stomach for a fight and the left – for it is mainly the left – is mobilising this discontent to mount a campaign for disengagement. If the United Kingdom were to disengage, Germany and other NATO countries would not perhaps be far behind and American political strategy would be in ruins.

The First Casualty

The Anti-War Party is not a party in the political sense: it is a coalition of pacifists, peaceniks, leftists, those who are always ready to beat the USA with a big stick and those who look at the situation in Afghanistan and become defeatist. We do not belong to the Anti-War coalition. We are aware, nevertheless, that the notion the Allies will be able, after a bloody military campaign, to leave behind a 'normalised', democratic Afghanistan, free from the Taliban, free from Al-Qaeda influence, with sufficient resources and appetite to police itself, tests credulity beyond all sensible bounds. Even if it were not corrupt, the Karzai administration in Kabul would never by itself be able to contain the Taliban. General Sir David Richards, head of the British army, admitted as much when he said in August 2009 that the British could be involved in Afghanistan for another thirty to forty years. Whether or not the Allies remain in Afghanistan, fighting an asymmetric war that neither side can win in the field, the war will continue. It will, perhaps, be fought in the streets of Paris, of London, of Jakarta, of Mumbai. With a global conflict looming, the calls of the Anti-War coalition to quit Afghanistan are almost irrelevant. What is certain, is that Pakistan will be involved – indeed, is heavily involved even as we write – and that the consequence of Pakistan's involvement will in many ways be crucial to the outcome.

◇

It is pertinent, therefore, to ask what has been the relationship between Pakistan and the Taliban? A connected question is why there are so many Taliban fighters within Pakistan itself not least in the Federally Administered Tribal Areas. With the withdrawal of the Soviets in 1989 the heroes of the moment were the *mujahideen* who had, with covert American, assistance done so much to harry the Russian invaders. But the popularity of the Afghan *mujahideen* dissipated with the passage of time. Gangs roamed the countryside, looting shops and committing other crimes. The area most affected was Kandahar, where the people sought relief from heroes who had in effect become bandits. The answer appeared to lie with a new force called the Taliban.

The world first became aware of the Taliban in 1994 when they were appointed by Islamabad to protect a convoy trying to open up a trade route between Pakistan and Central Asia. The group comprised of Afghans trained, along with former mujahideen, in religious schools in Pakistan. Later they captured Kandahar, beginning a remarkable advance that led to the capture of the capital Kabul in September 1996.

The aim and objectives of the Taliban were made clear: the restoration of peace in Afghanistan; disarming the local population; and implementing Sharia law. In an interview with the BBC, General Pervez Musharraf claimed that, 'Our national security compulsions as far as Afghanistan is concerned are, that the Pashtuns of Afghanistan have to be on Pakistan's side.' Pakistan's backing for the Taliban was explained in different ways.

The First Casualty

Some commentators saw it as Pakistan's relentless search for 'strategic depth' in the event of conventional war between India and Pakistan, while others pointed out that there were profits to be made from oil and gas pipelines from central to south Asia through a stable Afghanistan.

Circumstances change, however, and in politics, as in wars, yesterday's enemy can become today's friend. The presence of the Taliban in Pakistan became a matter of contention between Islamabad and the Americans and their allies. The Allies claimed the right to cross borders in pursuit of the Taliban but Pakistan countered by saying that its territorial integrity should not be compromised.

Following the US-led invasion of Afghanistan in 2001, Taliban and Al-Qaeda fighters fled into Pakistan's tribal area, especially Waziristan, spawning a Pakistani Taliban movement. Baitullah Mehsud was formally anointed head of the Taliban Movement of Pakistan in late 2007, although there remain Taliban groups that are not in his network.

By the middle of 2009, under pressure from the United States and concerned at terrorist attacks in its own cities, the Pakistan government - now led by Asif Ali Zardari, widower of Benazir Bhutto, with Yousaf Raza Gilani as his prime minister - decided to tackle the problems occasioned by the presence in the country of a large armed contingent that did not owe allegiance to Islamabad. The offensive risked engulfing the country in bloodshed as

The First Casualty

Baitullah Mehsud's terrorist network spans Pakistan, but the move seemed to finally signal that Islamabad is serious about fighting Islamic extremism and was expected to be welcomed by Western leaders.

Waziristan, which runs along the Afghan border, is a possible hiding place for Osama bin Laden. It is also a place where, according to the British intelligence services, many plots against Western targets are hatched. The governor of North West Frontier Province, Mr Owais Ghani, the top civilian official responsible for the tribal area, did not mince words: 'The military and law enforcement agencies have been ordered to carry out a full-fledged operation to eliminate these beasts and killers by using all resources'. He continued by stating that Baitullah Mehsud, leader of the Taliban in the region, 'is the root cause of all evils'. The move follows the Pakistan army's operation against a branch of Mehsud's Taliban network in the Swat valley, which started in late April. Waziristan, however, is a much tougher nut to crack. The terrain, as we have seen, is difficult and presents many problems to the Pakistan security forces launching an offensive. Pakistan is still struggling to cope with the displacement of about two million people from the Swat operation. Waziristan, in the northwest, could produce another half million refugees.

Baitullah Mehsud's group claimed three major terrorist attacks: the bombing of a luxury hotel in Peshawar, a blast at a mosque in Nowshera in the north west and the killing

The First Casualty

of an anti-Taliban cleric in the eastern city of Lahore. He is also suspected of masterminding the assassination of Benazir Bhutto, the former prime minister, in 2007.

By the middle of October 2009 the ground offensive, long in the planning and long delayed, was under way. But the Taliban had long expected the offensive and they struck back in the very heart of Pakistan, in Lahore, Peshawar and Rawalpindi, partly to parade their strength and partly to deflect attention from the government offensive. The attacks were audacious; the results greater than they dared have hoped for.

Ever since July the Pakistan army had been preparing for an attack on Taliban power in Waziristan held by Taliban, Uzbeks and Al-Qaeda fighters. In the build-up to a ground offensive, enemy areas had been relentlessly shelled by artillery, with support from jet aircraft. Roads had been sealed off, partly to make it easier for troop movements, partly to present the escape of militants. Many civilians had been unable to leave the areas but that is one of the results of modern warfare - civilians become caught up in hostilities. War, as we have noted before and as General William Tecumseh Sherman originally said in 1880, is hell.

Then Mehsud's Taliban struck. Within hours of leaving their camps early on Saturday morning to fight what is being hailed as the decisive battle in the war against terror, 12 soldiers had been killed in the first ferocious gunfights.

The First Casualty

Pakistan's generals have called the offensive the 'mother of all battles' for the survival of a country under siege. There were reports of Taliban compounds coming under aerial bombardment from Pakistan helicopter gunships as troops moved out in three columns from Razmak to the north, Jandola to the east and Shakai in the west and advanced on notorious Taliban target towns like Makeen and Ladha.

The significance of Pakistan's army having Makeen in its sights will not have been lost on Pakistan's president, Asif Zardari. The late Taliban leader, Baitullah Mehsud, was in Makeen when he was allegedly recorded on a telephone intercept claiming responsibility for the assassination of Mr Zardari's wife, Benazir Bhutto, the former Pakistan prime minister. This remote, dusty town close to the Afghan border had expected as much. It has for many months been the location chosen by the Americans for Predator drone attacks on Taliban commanders. It is in Makeen that there have been kidnappings of Pakistani troops and fierce gun battles between security forces and militants.

Thousands of residents had already fled the anticipated army assault and those who remained were under military curfew. The long-awaited army ground offensive had started. Long delayed, as army generals agonised over how the country would cope with the militant backlash that would inevitably follow. They had to weigh up the situation with great care. In fact, the backlash happened, as we have noted, even before the army assault.

The First Casualty

The breakthrough came late on Friday night when, in a highly unusual move, the Chief of Army Staff, General Ashfaq Kiyani, summoned all the main opposition party leaders to a meeting at the home of the prime minister, Yousuf Raza Gilani. Once assembled, they were asked for united support for what would be one of the army's most controversial operations: the use of overwhelming force against their own people – many of them tribal militants who had once been trained and encouraged by some of the leaders and generals now moving against them. But after one of the bloodiest weeks in recent history, in which Taliban fighters had stormed the Army's Rawalpindi headquarters and more than 160 people were killed by suicide bombers and commando-style gunmen, the generals and the politicians had little choice.

It was the beginning of this month of October 2009 when Sailab Mehsud, a local journalist covering Pakistan's dangerous tribal areas, received a call to meet the Taliban's new chief, Hakimullah Mehsud, at a secret location. (Hakimullah is a *nom de guerre*, but the Mehsud part is correct.) He was immediately sure he was on to a scoop: Hakimullah was supposed to be dead. According to Pakistani security forces, the militants' notorious 'boy general' – he is believed to be 28 years old or thereabouts– had been killed in a bitter succession battle with two rival Taliban commanders, Wali ur Rahman and Qari Hussain.

His 'death' had been a key factor in the army's preparations

The First Casualty

for a final assault. The Taliban had been wiped out in the Swat Valley, their South Waziristan leader, Baitullah Mehsud, had been killed in an American drone attack in August and now they were in disarray. Would there ever be a better time to launch a massive offensive? But when the handful of journalists summoned by the Taliban awoke after an overnight stop deep in South Waziristan on 4 October, following an 11 hour mountain and forest drive, they was greeted by the smiling face of the 'dead' man, brandishing an AK47 for the cameras and demonstrating with his laptop that he also has advanced computer skills.

'Tell the Pakistani government that I'm alive and determined to take severe revenge for Baitullah Mehsud's killing and the continued drone strikes,' Hakimullah, told the reporters, urging them to record his message on film. 'Both America and Pakistan will have to face the consequences. We have respect for Al-Qaeda and the jihadist organisations - we are with them.' He pledged to fulfil his predecessor's mission to destroy the Pakistani state for its 'collaboration' with the West and drown the country in blood.

Within hours of his interview being broadcast on 5th October - Mehsud had insisted on a delay to give him time to disappear - the boy general delivered on his threat, unleashing a wave of coordinated commando raids and suicide bombings which shattered army claims of Taliban disarray and destroyed the notion that they would be easy prey in their South Waziristan stronghold.

The First Casualty

The attacks began when a suicide bomber dressed as a paramilitary soldier tricked his way into a heavily guarded United Nations office in Islamabad and blew himself up, killing five UN employees. On 9 October a car bomb ripped through a busy market place in Peshawar, the capital of the North West Frontier Province, killing 53 people.

The tipping point, however, came in the third week of October 2009 when the Pakistani Taliban and its extremist allies demonstrated the scale of their ambition. A team of 10 gunmen attacked the army's General Headquarters in Rawalpindi, shooting their way through two gates to take 42 people hostage. In a 22-hour siege which was fought out live on television, 14 soldiers and civilian employees were killed along with all but one of the terrorists.

Such a brazen assault on the nerve centre of the country's military establishment heightened fears in Pakistan, and interested observers around the world, about the security of the country's nuclear weapons if the army could be humiliated like this in its own headquarters.

Was this the end of the brazen assaults? It seemed not; Mehsud was just getting into his stride. Within days a child suicide bomber, no older than 13 years, targeted a military convoy moving through a bazaar in Shangla, close to the Swat Valley in the North West Frontier Province. The blast killed all six soldiers in an army

The First Casualty

vehicle and 35 shoppers on the street. Another myth was exploded: the notion that the Taliban had been totally defeated in Swat.

Then came three simultaneous gun and explosives assaults in Pakistan's cultural and business capital, Lahore, in the heart of Punjab. Commandos struck at two police training centres and the office of the Federal Investigation Agency the national law enforcement body. The so-called 'swarm' attack was modelled on last year's 26 November attack on Mumbai, and the death toll could have matched it had it not been for a fight-back from local security forces that limited the deaths to 28.

Meanwhile in Kohat, back in the North-West frontier Province, another suicide bomber killed 11 on the same day when he rammed his car into a police station. Later that day, a car exploded outside a housing complex for government employees in Peshawar, killing a six-year-old boy and wounding nine others, including women and children.

On Friday the death toll climbed higher still when a car bomb exploded as it drove into the front of Peshawar's police intelligence headquarters. According to some reports - still unconfirmed - one of the attackers was a woman who jumped from a motorbike, unbuttoned her coat and detonated her suicide vest by a neighbouring government housing complex, killing thirteen. Half the police station being completely destroyed by the blast and

The First Casualty

the other half engulfed in flames while dazed police officers searched for their missing comrades in the rubble.

Ordinary Pakistanis have been left bewildered, unable still to believe that the danger comes from within the country. 'Only God knows where such people come from because I know that Muslims cannot kill other Muslims,' said Mohammad Yousaf, a 55-year-old, who runs a tea shop near one of the police training schools in Lahore and spent several hours hiding instead his store as gunfire and explosions engulfed the area.

This latest Taliban onslaught, waged by leaders who were supposed to be dead, has thoroughly shocked Pakistan. In fact, despite its omnipresent ISI intelligence agency and large standing army, it was the army that appeared to be in the greatest disarray. Its headquarters had been left poorly guarded despite several Taliban attacks on military centres in the last two years. The militants anticipated similar chaos when they decided to attack the same Lahore police training college they had laid siege to earlier in the year. They were not disappointed.

The Army's top brass was reported to be furious, not only with the failings of their own people, but also with their political leaders. The country's interior minister Rehman Malik was virtually banned from paying his respects to the dead at the army's GHQ by generals; they blamed him for leaking their plans for the imminent South Waziristan offensive. Such leaks were of serious import. They gave

The First Casualty

warning to Taliban fighters, as well as Uzbek militants, Arabs and Mehsud tribesmen, who moved into neighbouring Orakzai in order to escape the military onslaught and thus live to fight another day. Not all fled, however; some stayed behind to put up a fight. An army convoy was bombed at Razmak, several soldiers were killed or wounded at Sarwakay and more were injured in a gun battle at Spinkay Raghzay. But the main battle was yet to be engaged.

For Pakistan's allies in the war on terror the army offensive may not materially assist their struggle against the Taliban across the border in Afghanistan. The army is targeting Taliban fighters from the Mehsud tribe, which have allied themselves with Al-Qaeda in attacking Pakistan's military institutions. But the offensive is not expected to target the Haqqani network, a branch of the Taliban which has mounted some of the worst attacks on NATO forces in Afghanistan. Nor will it take on other pro-Afghan Taliban faction that support Mullah Omar's call for militants to focus their attacks on Western forces rather than the Pakistani military.

Some observers blame Pakistan's ties with the United States; the jihadists now see no difference between Americans and the Pakistan army. There are fears that the alliance with the United States will lead to the destruction of Pakistan as a state, little more than sixty years after its foundation at the partitioning of the sub-continent. To add substance to this claim is the knowledge that jihadists are

The First Casualty

not only in Waziristan, but are to be found in Punjab, Balochistan and in Sindh. On how many fronts can the Pakistan army fight? Does it have the means to subdue its own Taliban rebels, to fight Afghan Taliban taking shelter in its country and also keep control of Kashmir?

When General Ashfaq Kayani called together members of the cabinet and leaders of opposition parties on 16 October 2009, he warned them to brace themselves for an unprecedented terrorist backlash. Without doubt, as the general made abundantly clear, Pakistan as a state is fighting for its very existence.

The taking of South Waziristan, which will not be achieved in days and may take many months, is important for several reasons. It is the main refuge for militants from Afghanistan. It also has numerous training camps for suicide bombers. Then, most important perhaps for Pakistan within its region, it is destabilizing Pakistan itself. Yet it is no easy decision for a general to issue orders for his soldiers to open fire on their own people.

As we have tried repeatedly to stress, there are no easy answers. The fulcrum is Pakistan, Allied forces need to understand they cannot afford another destabilized state in this region and certainly not one that has nuclear weapons and a large population. A destabilised Pakistan will be more dangerous for the world than a destabilised Afghanistan. The Allied effort must take Pakistan into account, not as a client state, but as a full player in a sub-

The First Casualty

continental drama that is being played out in the cockpit of Asia. More than the outcome of the battle for South Waziristan is at stake. More than the future government of Afghanistan is at stake. Policy of making a new government in Afghanistan needs to be purely on the ratio of ethnicity with Pashtuns as the major players. The stability and future of Pakistan itself and its place within the sub-continent are also of supreme importance.

What is going on is a proxy war, fought out on Afghanistan soil. There have always been proxy wars, not least in Africa during the Cold War. Now, with the end of the Cold War, new alliances have been formed, based on the conflicting interests of regional powers. To begin with the Taliban received support from Pakistan, Saudi Arabia and the UAE, while Iran, Russia and India have supported and continue to support, the Northern Alliance. As a result, an already war-torn country continues to bleed. To take an example, and there are many to choose from: after Masoud's assassination, the vice president of Afghanistan became the main conduit for India's overt and covert assistance to the Northern Alliance in its struggle against the Taliban. Another of India's friends in the interim administration included Foreign Minister Abdullah Abdullah – currently challenging Karzai for the presidency; Interior Minister Younus Qanooni and Taj Muhammad Wardak. It has always been India's policy to have as much control as possible over events on its northern frontiers.

The First Casualty

While the Taliban were in control of Afghanistan, India strove to form a common front with Iran, Russia and the Central Asian Republics against the religiously inspired 'terrorism' purportedly being propagated by Pakistan and the Taliban. India's intention has always been to reduce Pakistan's role in Central Asia. The policy has been known as the North-South Corridor Agreement, connecting Moscow and Tehran. As the United States has always considered Central American to be its own 'backyard', so India too – and from another direction, Russia – has always considered that it is politic to keep Pakistan unstable and without alliances in the region. In Afghanistan, defence and foreign affairs remain in the firm grip of the Northern Alliance. In the event of another war with India, Pakistan cannot expect any diplomatic or material support from its neighbours.

Anyone who questions the extent of Indian influence and meddling in Afghanistan need only consider the fact that there are many Indian consulates in the eastern cities of Afghanistan along Pakistan's western border. These pose a serious threat to the internal security of Pakistan in the form of support for sectarianism and terrorism.

It is to India's advantage to fan prolonged insurgency and lawlessness in the FATA and Balochistan regions, those parts of Pakistan contiguous with Afghanistan. The fact that several members of the present Afghan government, including Hamid Karzai himself, have close links with India does not bode well for Afghanistan or for Pakistan.

The First Casualty

The situation in the region is much more tangled than the general public in western nations are led to believe.

The costs of the recent and comprehensive defeat in Afghanistan are yet to be calculated, but according to one assessment, the current war in Afghanistan is expected to inflict a direct cost on the Pakistan economy of some US $ 4 billion. This is a burden too heavy to be borne alone and yet U.S. aid to Pakistan, in so far as is made public, is derisory in comparison.

Another disquieting development for Pakistan is the nexus forged between India and Iran. Nobody in the West should be lulled into believing that Iran is a friendless or pariah nation. Historically and currently, Iran has long had relations with and influence upon Afghanistan and since 1947 this meddling has usually been against the interests of Pakistan.

If Pakistan were to fall as a united nation - and this is always a possibility given the forces ranged against it, the very forces to whom it would be advantageous to have a partitioned and warring Pakistan - it would lead to regional conflicts compared with which the present events in Afghanistan would appear to be merely a prelude.

◇

Currently, even as we write, events are unfolding in South Waziristan which are crucial for the future of the region.

The First Casualty

The Pakistan government, as we have shown, finally moved in a land and air offensive against the Taliban within its own country. It has been said that the Pakistan government is bombarding its own people but this is only partially true. The Taliban elements within Pakistan act as enemies of the state. As the ground forces of the Pakistan army moved deeper into Waziristan the Taliban would be crushed, it was believed, between the advancing troops and the American and ISAF troops to the north, effectively cutting off all escape.

However, there are disquieting reports to the contrary and not only issuing from Islamabad. It has been reliably reported that US-led NATO forces vacated more than half a dozen key security check posts on the Afghan side of the Pakistan-Afghan border just ahead of the major Pakistan Army ground offensive (code named: Ra he Nijaat) against Taliban-led militants in the volatile tribal area of South Waziristan. It is feared that the American decision will facilitate not only possible escape for the Mehsud clan and the Taliban, but also allow the Afghan Taliban to cross over to Pakistan to support militants, thus making it harder for the Pakistan army to deal effectively, once and for all, with insurgents in the troubled tribal areas.

Sources close to the North West Frontier Province government, as well as military intelligence, reported that at least eight security checkpoints had been vacated. Pakistan is not wrong to wonder who are its friends. The decision to vacate was not sudden, but taken five days before the launch of the long-expected ground offensive. Four of the posts left unguarded are close to South Waziristan including one each at Zambezi and at Nurkha, and four in the north in the area of Nuristan where American forces recently came under strong and persistent attack by the militants.

What we wonder, and so to doubtless the Pakistan government and military, are American designs? What is the nature of these dubious decisions? That they have caused astonishment in the area, cannot be denied. However, when the US Embassy spokesman in Islamabad, Richard Snelsire, was contacted and his attention drawn to the question of vacated check posts he remained non-committal. 'I do not have information on that, and that is outside our purview,' he replied. We can only surmise, until reliable evidence is produced, that the American government of President Obama wants to reduce some of the intense pressure from its own troops and thus reduce casualty figures. It is casualty figures that most trouble public opinion in western countries. Such figures are one of the true pieces of evidence of how the war in Afghanistan is progressing. In the meantime, 28,000 Pakistan soldiers are meeting fierce resistance from the heavily armed Taliban-led militants and Pakistan is also taking casualties, though these are not usually reported in the western media.

Recent communication intercepts by Pakistani intelligence sources have revealed that the Taliban commander in

The First Casualty

Nuristan, Qari Ziaur Rehman, has invited Maulvi Faqir Mohammad, former deputy of late Baitullah Mehsud, to come to Nuristan and operate from there if he finds that his operational space in Wazristan is shrinking because of advances by government troops. Such movement of resources would not be too difficult, given the removal of border crossing security. The Pakistan operation is further in danger of being undermined. It must be remembered, the Taliban receives support from foreign elements – Uzbeks, Chechen, Tajiks, Arabs even – and, of course, Al-Qaeda. This further mystifies those who remember that the war started with the Americans declaring their target to be Al-Qaeda and *Operation Enduring Freedom,* the means of removing Al-Qaeda as a fighting force. This is not the place to delve deeper into the success or otherwise of that operation, but the Americans are admitting that 70 per cent of Afghanistan is out of their control. It would not be against Allied interests in the short term to move the theatre of operations into the tribal areas of Pakistan.

War is not merely a military opportunity. In all wars, in all the ages, there is also the involvement of criminal elements. This is true of South Waziristan. The uninterrupted flow of sophisticated arms and funding to the foreign militants has also lured many criminals to join hands with them in challenging the writ of the state, according to defence experts. The presence of various foreign and local militants in the rugged terrain of South Waziristan is estimated at between 15,000 and 20,000.

The First Casualty

The outcomes are not certain, but officials in the military and civil bureaucracy of Pakistan are cautiously optimistic. 'Either these militants will run to Afghanistan, settled areas or stand and fight to the end,' is how one key NWFP government representative summed up the situation. A key office holder in Peshawar, the military centre of Pakistan, states: 'We are half way in containing insurgency and hopefully by end of the year major military operations will be over and 2010 will be the year of consolidating the gains made in recovering the lost ground.' That is a realistic and sensible assessment. Whatever the outcome, observers believe that the military operation in the Taliban stronghold of South Waziristan became inevitable. 'It became imperative to go for a military operation in South Waziristan to regain the lost space that has been used as training ground for planning and executing attacks targeting key security installations of Pakistan including the GHQ,' the Army spokesman Major General Athar Abbas said shortly after the launch of the operation.

This is not the end of the state of Pakistan formed in 1947 but it is in many ways its greatest test. And the future of Pakistan is inextricably bound to the future of Afghanistan. Of that there should be no doubt in anybody's mind.

The First Casualty

THE AUTHORS

John Adam and M.A. Akbar

The authors, John Adam and M.A. Akbar, answer the fundamental questions people all over the world are constantly asking: Who are the Taliban? How are they connected, if at all, to Al Qaeda? Can the West win the war in Afghanistan? What has been going on there since 2001? Why are the top military forces failing and what are the lessons for them? Who are the stakeholders and how can this issue be resolved?

In this timely and important book the authors, who know the region well, show why Afghanistan is the cockpit of Asia. They write from their own experience of the many peoples of the area and a close interest in the history and politics of Afghanistan. This concise book gets right to the point and tells us all what we need to know. Nobody could have produced a better account.

"'In war, truth is the first casualty'. Thus wrote Aeschylus, the Greek dramatist, two and a half thousand years ago. It was true then; it is true now. Separating truth from propaganda is never easy but in this book we are trying to get at the facts", John Adam and M.A. Akbar.

The First Casualty

ALSO AVAILABLE FROM

STRAND PUBLISHING

Non-fiction

- The Strand Book of International Poets 2010
- The Strand Book of Short Stories 2010
- The Strand Book of Memorable Maxims
  (Suggestions for this series are welcome)

- The Challenge of Reality by Sultan Bashir Mahmood
- The First Casualty by John Adam and MA Akbar

Fiction

- The Path of the Gods by Joseph Geraci

All titles are available online and through retail outlets.

For further information visit: www.strandpublishing.co.uk
and follow the links at the top of the Home Page.

The First Casualty

STRAND PUBLISHING UK LTD

For further information about what we publish visit our website: www.strandpublishing.co.uk.

Submissions are always welcome, in all genres.

Follow our submission guidelines on our website: www.strandpublishing.co.uk
or email at: info@strandpublishing.co.uk

We are looking for short books on controversial subjects.

If you have written such a book, or plan to write one, please drop us an email.

Or you may wish to contribute to the 'The Strand Book ……' series. All serious suggestions welcome.

We welcome all enquiries from authors and/or their agents.

Our sole criterion is that all submissions must be written in English, British or American version.

www.ingramcontent.com/pod-product-compliance
Lightning Source LLC
Chambersburg PA
CBHW031256110426

42743CB00039B/625